THE WORLD OF FLOWERS IN WOOL

Lily Simons

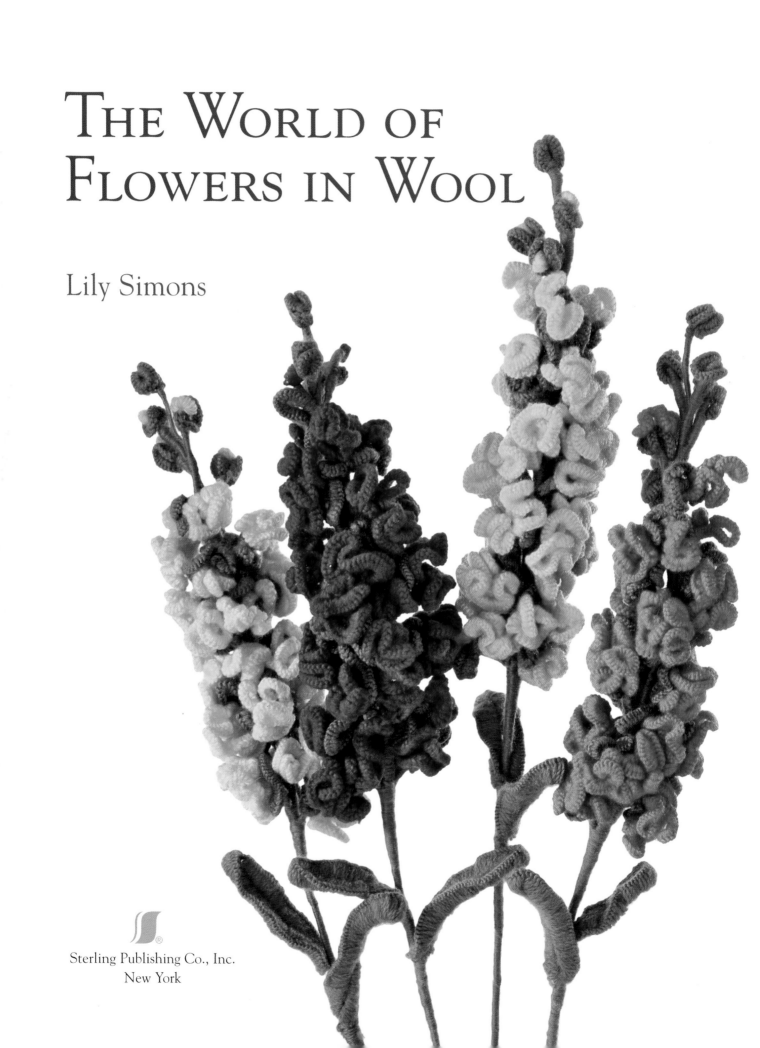

Sterling Publishing Co., Inc.
New York

Photographs by Michael Hnatov

Library of Congress Cataloging-in-Publication Data

Simons, Lily, 1923-
    The world of flowers in wool / Lily Simons.
      p. cm.
    Includes index.
    ISBN-13: 978-1-4027-2488-6
    ISBN-10: 1-4027-2488-8
    1. Artificial flowers. 2. Knitting.   I. Title.
  TT890.S44 2006
  745.594'3—dc22

                        2006013719

10 9 8 7 6 5 4 3 2 1

Published by Sterling Publishing Co., Inc.
387 Park Avenue South, New York, NY 10016
©2006 by Lily Simons
Distributed in Canada by Sterling Publishing
⁒ Canadian Manda Group, 165 Dufferin Street
Toronto, Ontario, Canada M6K 3H6
Distributed in the United Kingdom by GMC Distribution Services
Castle Place, 166 High Street, Lewes, East Sussex, England BN7 1XU
The Chrysalis Building, Bramley Road, London W10 6SP, England
Distributed in Australia by Capricorn Link (Australia) Pty. Ltd.
P.O. Box 704, Windsor, NSW 2756, Australia

Printed in China
Sterling ISBN-13: 978-1-4027-2488-6
        ISBN-10: 1-4027-2488-8

For information about custom editions, special sales, premium and
corporate purchases, please contact Sterling Special Sales
Department at 800-805-5489 or specialsales@sterlingpub.com.

Contents

BASICS

Flowers are miracles that have been written about in stories and poems, carved in stone, modeled in clay, painted on canvas, copied in mosaics, and woven in fabric. I have been mesmerized by the millions of flowers from all over the world: flowers that can stand icy cold winter, flowers that can bloom in the heat of the desert, flowers that have fiestas and flowers with faces following the sun. I decided to try to imitate them in order to preserve at least a ghost of their presence. I began to take an interest in botanical textbooks, which eventually led me to various kinds of flower-making techniques. None of them satisfied me. I wanted a new method of flower-making, one which was simple to follow, which did not need complicated equipment or expensive working materials, and above all one which could produce flowers that looked true to nature in a relatively short period of time.

My search began to take shape. I arrived at a new method of flower-making that encompassed the above-mentioned qualities. The technique is so surprisingly simple that you might wonder why you didn't invent it yourself. Once you begin to experiment, you will soon discover what unlimited possibilities this technique can offer.

Throughout this book, you will find a wealth of ideas and numerous tips on how to achieve a professional look. I hope this book will be an inspiration to you and will provide you with a treasury of new creations of your own. Here are some points to watch out for when you create new flowers:

- Don't try to meticulously scrutinize every detail. Just squint your eyes a little and try to see the characteristics of the flowers. What attracts your attention? Forms, colors? Write them down: no memory is better than a scribble on paper.
- Don't worry about exact measurements. Judge the relative color and shape. Make a simple statement of your own.

I sincerely wish you many enjoyable and satisfying hours of flower-making.

Tools and Materials

The Stick and the Rubber Band

The stick is the major tool with which we create all the beautiful flowers in this book.

- We can easily make a working stick ourselves from a flat wooden stick 11¾" long and ⅛" thick (30 cm long and 0.4 cm thick).
- Take a stick that is one of the widths listed below. At one end of the stick, whittle both edges to a slanting point (Fig. 1-1).
- Cut a notch at the very top of the point. The purpose of this notch is to hook one end of the florist wire to the stick.
- Sandpaper the whole stick to a very smooth finish and then wax it.
- Repeat the above for each stick, preparing a number of sticks of different widths: ³⁄₁₆" (0.5 cm), ¼" (0.7 cm), ⁵⁄₁₆" (0.8 cm), ⅜" (1.0 cm), ½" (1.3 cm), ⅝" (1.5 cm), ¾" (2.0 cm), 1" (2.5 cm) and 1½" (4.0 cm). Label each one of them with its width.
- To use, hook a florist wire into the notch. Wind a rubber band around the untapered end of the stick to hold the florist wire in place.

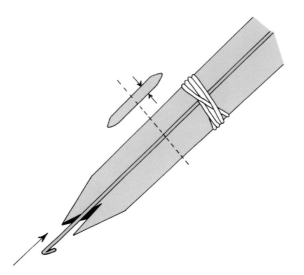

1-1. A whittled stick, showing point and florist wire. We begin by hooking the wire to the notch on the stick. Wind a rubber band around the other end of the stick to hold the wire in place. The wire stays on the stick while you are putting on your loops. The wire will transport and hold the loops by itself later on. Top oval shows cross-section of stick, which is 0.4 cm thick.

The Knitting Needle and Rubber Stop

- Collect an assortment of knitting needles of various sizes:

    US 8 (UK 6; 5 mm)
    US 9 (UK 5; 5.5 mm)
    US 10 (UK 4; 6 mm)
    US 10½ (UK 3; 6.5 mm)

- Take a rubber stop, normally used to keep the knitting from falling off the needle while we are not working on it. Cut the head off the stop (Fig. 1-2a).

- Sandpaper its base until it is slightly rounded. The function of this rubber stop is identical with that of the notch in the stick: to keep one end of the florist wire secured at the needle tip.

- To use the knitting needle, secure one end of the florist wire with the stop. Wind a rubber band around the other end of the needle to secure the other end of the wire (Fig. 1-2b).

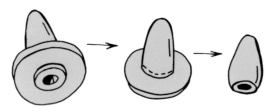

1-2a. Modifying a knitting needle stop, which will serve to secure the florist wire on a knitting needle.

1-2b. The wire, fitted into a knitting needle stop and secured with a rubber band, will be held in place on the needle while stitches are cast on.

Other Tools and Supplies

You will need scissors, pliers that can cut wire, a tapestry or yarn needle with a big eye, a ruler, and a crochet hook. Below we describe some other supplies you will need.

Wool or Yarn

If you live in the U. S., you probably call it yarn. In the U. K. it's called wool. We'll use both terms interchangeably in the book. As working wool, we use ordinary knitting yarn. Because real sheep's wool is expensive, you can use synthetic wool, even though we will refer to it as "wool." The flowers in this book were made from a double strand of two-ply low-twist yarn (I was really working with 4 strands at a time).

However, you may have to adjust the number of plies, depending on your yarn. You may not need to double the yarn. Do a test leaf or petal before starting a flower, to see how your yarn works. Stems may be wrapped with either a single or a double strand of wool, as circumstances require. Microfiber yarn works well for stems. A single strand of yarn wound around the wire produces a thinner stem. To divide the yarn, get a friend to help you and each take a few strands and roll them into 2 separate balls. Here are some other likely brands and kinds of wool to use for flowers: Sayelle® 4-ply orlon/acrylic knitting yarn; Wintuk acrylic worsted yarn; Mary Maxim® yarns; Pinguin worsted yarn. For some flowers, such as bouvardia and forget-me-not, we use undivided yarn, rather than splitting it into 2-ply parts. This will be noted in the projects.

Photo 1. Supplies for making wool flowers.

Sewing Thread

Unless noted otherwise in the instructions, always use sewing thread of the same color as whatever you are working on, so it is not noticeable. You might use thread to tie flower petals to a stem or attach leaves to a twig. A contrasting color of thread will spoil the whole effect. If a contrasting color of thread is needed, it will be specifically mentioned in the instructions.

Stamens

In most cases we use ready-made stamens (Photo 2), available from floral supply stores, but sometimes we need to make stamens from yarn or thread. See each project for details.

Glue

Flower-making adhesive needs to be strong and transparent when dry. A good choice is a polyvinyl acetate (PVAc) adhesive, commonly known as white glue. Proprietary brands such as UHU All-Purpose Crafts Glue and Elmer's Glue-All

Photo 2. Ready-made stamens around the center of a water lily.

are two examples. UHU is a fast-drying glue, used for tipping the ends of wool to prevent it from unwinding. PVAc glue needs some time to set. It is also very useful for attaching calyxes to flowers.

Wire

The petals and leaves are transferred from the stick onto wire in most cases. The wire, bent into shape, becomes the support of the wool of the leaves, petals, etc. Special florist wire, used in flower-making, comes in different thicknesses, ranging from #18 to #30; the higher the number, the thinner the wire.

Soft, fine ordinary general-purpose galvanized wire can substitute the more expensive florist wire. It is flexible and comes in a roll, so it can be cut to any length you need. Use thin florist wire for flower petals and thicker wire for the leaves, except when the flower petals are very long or very large, in which case use the heavier wire for the petals as well. For thicker stems, use all-purpose galvanized wire that is thicker and more rigid, about gauge 16 to 14 (.06" to .08" or 1.5 to 2 mm). Use the heavier gauge (2 mm) for heavy main stems.

Florist Tape

Florist tape is made from a self-adhesive, crepelike material. It is frequently used on stems. It should be stretched when used. Keep the tape taut while winding it down the stem. The tape is sold in various sizes and colors (green, black, brown, white) and comes mostly in ½" (1.3 cm) wide rolls. Florist tape is indispensable for several reasons:

- It gives a surer grip to the winding wool added on top of it on stems, etc.
- Wrapped around the stem before winding with wool, florist tape will soften the angular bulges caused by wires and bindings.
- Florist tape will give the final product a neat, professional appearance.

Tissue Paper

Tissue paper is used to pad the stem, when we need a thick one. Wrap the stem with tissue paper first; then wrap with florist tape before winding it with wool, to obtain a smooth surface.

The Basic Method

The Smooth-Edge Method of Casting on Loops

- Hook one end of the florist wire onto the notch in the stick and fasten the other end with a rubber band.
- Before you start, leave a tail of wool, which will be the assisting wool (see Note about the Assisting Wool on page 12).
- For the first stitch, make a slip knot (loop) as in Fig. 1-3a, and transfer the loop to the stick.
- With slip knot on stick, wrap assisting and working yarns around fingers as shown, ready to form the next loop (Fig. 1-3a).
- Proceed step by step as indicated in Figs. 1-3b, 1-3c, and 1-3d. Specifically:
- Insert the stick through the thumb loop and rotate tip of stick to the right, over the loop on index finger (Fig. 1-3b).

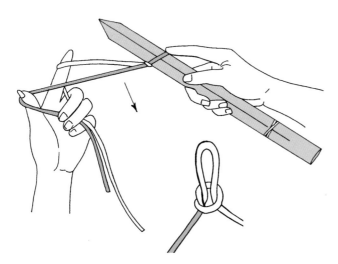

I-3a. The smooth-edge method of casting on stitches, Step 1. To start, make a loop of wool and transfer it to the stick as the first loop, with the unattached end of wool dangling about 8 times the length of the loops that you will be putting on the stick. The dangling wool is called the assisting wool (shown in red in these diagrams for clarity). Nearby, a closeup of a loop off the stick.

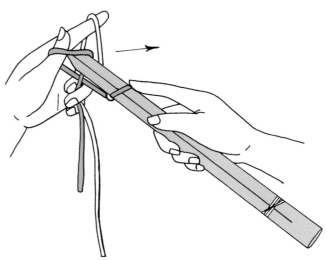

I-3b. The smooth-edge method, Step 2. With the left hand, separate the two strands of thread to thumb and index finger, opening the fingers in a V. Bring the stick down to pick up the wool. Both strand end (assisting wool and main wool) are held between fingers as shown to regulate tension.

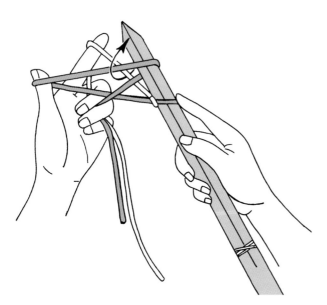

I-3c. The smooth-edge method, Step 3. Pass the stick under the red wool and pull farther up.

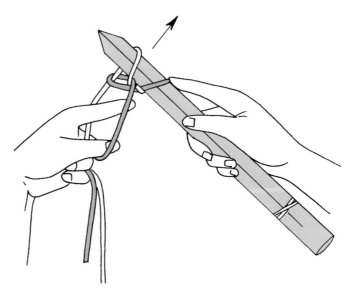

I-3d. The smooth-edge method, Step 4. Pass the stick under and around the white wool to make the second loop. To tighten the loop we drop the red wool and at the same time open the thumb and index finger in a letter V. Keep making more loops this way.

- Rotate stick under index finger loop and over thumb loop to wrap and draw a new loop onto stick (Fig. 1-3c).
- Tighten the working and assisting yarn at the base of the new loop (Fig. 1-3d).
- The length of the loop section on the stick is the distance from the first to the last loop, shown in Fig. 1-3e. Keep casting on loops in the same way as described above, until you have the required amount of loops; this is usually referred to in the projects as the "length of loops on the stick" for whatever you are trying to make: a petal, a leaf, etc. The length of the loops for each is given in the project instructions.
- Once you have put the desired length of loops on the stick, make a loose knot at the end of the loops to secure them (Fig. 1-3e).

Note About the Assisting Wool: The white wool in the diagrams given here is the working wool, which is connected to the ball of wool. The assisting wool is colored red in the diagrams so you can see it clearly. It is the tail of wool you leave at the beginning before you start making loops. For the smooth-edge petals, calyxes, and leaves, the assisting wool should be about 8 times the length of the loops you will put on the stick (measured with the loops closed up together on the stick). For example, if you need to make a ¾" (2 cm) length of loops on the stick for a leaf or petal, your assisting wool tail should be 6" (16 cm) long; that is, ¾" × 8 (or 2 cm × 8). It is better to be a little generous and allow extra wool beyond the estimated 8 times the length of the loops for the assisting wool. Nothing is more annoying than having to undo the loops you have made because you ran out of assisting wool.

- See How to Make Petals and Leaves with Smooth Edges (page 22) to find out how to proceed after that.

On pages 13 and 14 are two variations of the smooth-edge method: one for leaves, calyxes, and petals with frilled edge and one done on a knitting needle to create narrow leaves, calyxes, and petals.

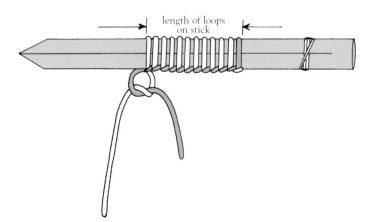

1-3e. The smooth-edge method, Step 5. After you have made enough loops to be the correct length of loops on the stick (distance between the arrows) when closed up together on the stick, cut the wool off the ball, leaving a tail, and tie the two wool ends together below the stick.

The Frilled-Edge Method of Casting On Loops

For the frilled-edge method, the assisting wool should be 10 times as long as the desired length of the loops on the stick.

- Hook one end of the florist wire onto the notch in the stick. Make a slip knot (loop) as in Fig. 1-3a. Transfer the loop to the stick.
- Work as for the smooth-edge method until there are 3 loops on the stick (Fig. 1-4a).
- Add 3 more loops on the stick, but begin them about ⅝"(1.5 cm) away from the last loop. Keep adding loops in threes (Fig. 1-4b).
- Slide the 3 loops back on the stick to touch the earlier loops, letting the excess yarn at the bottom of the loops bunch up (Fig. 1-4c).
- Keep adding groups of 3 loops to the stick as many times as needed, until the required number of loops (= the length of loops on the stick) is reached.
- Cut the working yarn off the ball, leaving a 3" (7.5 cm) end.
- Loosely knot the ends of the working and assisting yarns together.
- See How to Make Petals and Leaves with Frilled Edges (page 23) to find out how to proceed after that.

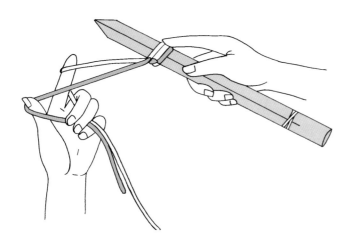

1-4a. The frilled-edge method of casting on loops. To start cast on 3 loops as with the smooth-edge method (Steps 1 to 4) until you have three loops on the stick. Leave a tail of wool that is 10 times the desired length of loops for the assisting wool.

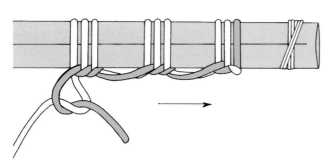

1-4b. Frilled-edge loops when cast on in groups of threes will look like this on the stick about ⅝" (1.5 cm) apart.

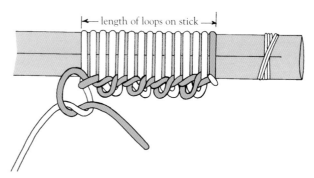

length of loops on stick

1-4c. Frilled-edge method, with stitches closed up to the length of loops on stick you need (distance between arrows). Cut off the length of wool attached to the ball, leaving a long tail, and make a knot with the assisting and main wool.

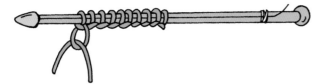

1-5a. Stitches on a knitting needle (wool ends have been tied); stop and rubber band are holding wire in place.

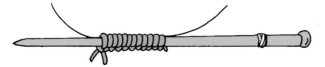

1-5b. Stop and rubber band have been removed from the wire.

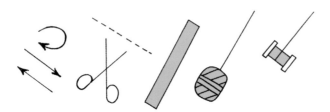

1-6. Symbols used in book. Left to right: arrows, which indicate direction of action or point of attention; cut here with scissors; use florist tape to cover the wire; use wool for winding; use sewing thread to tie or bind together.

The Knitting Needle Method

Up to now we have used a stick as a tool, but sticks are not suitable for extremely narrow petals or leaves. For this purpose we need knitting needles. They are also used for leafed calyxes.

- Collect an assortment of knitting needles of various sizes.
- Prepare a rubber stop for each (see Fig. 1-2a).
- Secure one end of the florist wire by putting the stop over the needle tip.
- Wind a rubber band around the other end of the needle (Fig. 1-2b).
- The rest of the method of making loops with a knitting needle is exactly the same as making loops on a stick. Fig. 1-5a and Photo 3 show some loops on a knitting needle.
- After you have prepared the loops, bend the ends of the wire up to hold them (Fig. 1-5b).
- Slide the wire and its loops from the needle, and twist the loop section to make a calyx, leaf, or petal shape as needed.

Symbols

Some symbols are used in the diagrams. Their meanings are given in Fig. 1-6.

Photo 3. Loops cast on a knitting needle; the stop and rubber band are still in place.

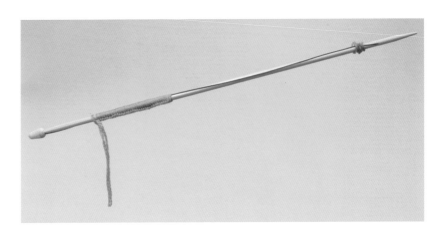

Flowers 101

Here is some basic leaf and flower terminology so you will be able to easily understand how the flowers are put together. If possible, study actual plants so you can learn more about them.

Kinds of Leaf

simple leaves: Simple leaves are made up of a single part or blade on a stem; an oak leaf is an example.

compound leaves: Compound leaves are divided into several small leaflets attached to the same leaf stalk. An example is the rose leaf shown in Photo 4. Some compound leaves have several lobes, like the clover.

Attachment of a Leaf to a Main Stem

Leaves are attached to stems in a variety of ways. Many leaves have a little stem (petiole) that attaches the leaf to a main stem. Some leaves don't have the petioles but attach directly to a stem or branch (Photo 5).

Photo 4. These roses have compound leaves, made up of small leaflets.

Photo 5. These leaves attach to a stem without having leaf stems (petioles). At left, a detached leaf.

Here are some typical arrangements of leaves on a stem:

opposite: Leaves exactly opposite each other on the stem. Example: bouvardia (Photo 6).

alternate: Leaves out of step with each other on opposite sides of the stem. Example: African daisy (Photo 7).

whorled: Leaves arranged around each other at the same height on a stem. Example: frangipani (Photo 8).

Photo 6. Leaves in opposite pattern on bouvardia.

Photo 8. Whorled arrangement of leaves on frangipani.

Photo 7. Leaves in alternate pattern on African daisy.

Inflorescence

Inflorescence is the characteristic arrangement of flowers on a stem. Here are some typical inflorescences:

solitary: One flower with no leaves on the stem (example: tulip).

simple umbel: (From Latin, *umbella*, a parasol.) A number of flower stalks, nearly equal in length, spread from a common center. Examples: geranium (Photo 9), agapanthus.

compound umbel: Arrangement with many groups of little umbels. Example: bouvardia (see Photo 6).

corymb: a flat-topped cluster of flowers, in which all the blooms end up at about the same height, because their stalks off the main stem are of different lengths. Example: statice.

simple raceme: *Racemus* is Latin for "cluster of grapes." Each flower is on a small stalk (pedicel) that arises off a central stem. Example: lily of the valley, yellow loosestrife (Photo 10).

panicle: Arrangement with loose, diversely branching flower clusters. There are short floral stalks on secondary branches off the main stem. Example: crape myrtle (Photo 11).

spike: The flower heads arise directly from the central stem. Example: snapdragon (Photo 12).

flower head (capitulum): The flower head looks like a single flower with many petals. It's really a dense, compact cluster of small flowers. Two examples: chrysanthemum and sunflower.

Calyx

Under the flower or bud, we frequently have a calyx, a supporting structure made up of leaflike parts called sepals. Originally the sepals protected the flower bud. The calyx is usually green. There are several kinds, as will be explained later.

Photo 9. The flowers of the geranium are arranged in an umbrella-like umbel.

Photo 10. Yellow loosestrife has flowers arranged in a simple raceme.

Photo 11. Crape myrtle has flowers arranged in a panicle.

Photo 12. Snapdragon carries flowers in a spike arrangement.

More Techniques

NOTE TO READER:

The following section, through Formula 4 on page 21, explains how to calculate the sizes of flower parts, which might be helpful if you are making new flower designs of your own or if you are adjusting the directions to your wool size. However, as the stick width and leaf and petal size are included in the project directions, you can skip the following section of formulas and continue with How to Make Petals and Leaves with Smooth Edges on page 22 if you wish.

What Width Stick to Use

The width of the stick you will need depends on the size and shape of the petal or leaf. The project directions indicate which width of sticks to use for a leaf, petal, etc. The illustrations below

will show you how to determine the proper stick width. This is helpful when you want to make a wool flower not shown in this book, or if you want to make a smaller or larger one than the version shown.

- First we draw a life-size sketch of the desired leaf form on paper (Fig. 1-7a).
- Measure half the width of the leaf; use its widest side if the sides are uneven (see Fig. 1-7b for schematic of leaf). Half the width of the leaf is RS, which will also be the width of the stick we need.
- Please keep in mind that the finished product will be slightly larger than the actual size we intended, due to the loss of tension in the wool, when the loops are removed from the stick.
- In order to make leaves of uniform length, keep a tape measure or a marked strip of paper on the table for reference.

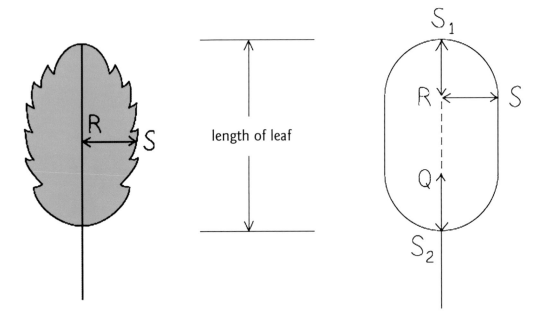

1-7a. Determining stick width (RS) on a real leaf. RS = half the width of the leaf.

1-7b. A basic leaf diagram with some measurements marked on it. RS = half a leaf. RQ = center of leaf. Distance S_1 to S_2 = total length of leaf.

How Many Loops (Length of Loops) to Put on the Stick

The length of loops on the stick is the measurement from the first to the last loop, when they are all slid close to each other on the stick (Fig. 1-7c). We have several formulas to calculate how many loops to use, depending on the size and shape of the leaf, calyx, or petal. However, this has been all figured out already for you in the project.

How can we get the amount of loops we need for a particular leaf, petal, etc.? You could put a number of loops on the stick and see how many you have in a centimeter or an inch. Then you could add the loops you need by counting, but that might be tiresome, so just put on a lot of loops close together on the stick, measuring the amount from time to time with a ruler, until you get to the required length of loops on the stick. You could also mark the stick with inches or centimeters.

Formula 1, For Leaf or Petal Length Above 2" (5 cm)

In Formula 1 leaves, the length of loops on stick = 2RQ + RS

> where RS is the width of the stick (half the width of the leaf or petal)
>
> and RQ is the center of the leaf.
>
> RQ = the total leaf length – 2RS
>
> Note that RS = RS_1 = QS_2 (see Fig. 1-7b).
>
> The total length of the leaf or petal is from S_1 to S_2 in our diagram.

Formula 1 example: Let's say we need a petal ¾" (2 cm) wide and 3⅛" (8 cm) long. We need a stick half the width of the petal, or ⅜" (1 cm) = RS.

> The length of loops to put on the stick for Formula 1 = 2RQ + RS
>
> To calculate RQ in inches: RQ = 3⅛" – 2RS = 2⅜"
>
> in cm: RQ = 8 cm – 2 (1 cm) = 6 cm

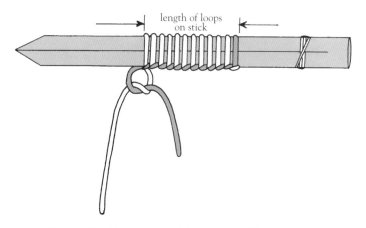

1-7c. The length of loops on a stick is measured from the first to the last loop (distance between arrows).

In this case, the length of loops on the stick to make the Formula 1 petal should be:

> in inches: 2RQ + RS = 2 (2⅜") + ⅜" = 5⅛"
>
> in cm: 2RQ + RS = 2 (6 cm) + 1 cm = 13 cm

Tulips are an example of long leaves made with Formula 1 (Photo 13).

Photo 13. Tulips have long leaves, made with Formula 1.

Photo 14. Cat-tail leaves were made using Formula 2.

Now that we know RQ, we can calculate the length of the loops on stick required for Formula 2 = 2RQ + 2RS

in inches = 2 (1") + 2 (3/8") = 2¾"

in cm: 2 (2.5 cm) + 2 (1 cm) = 7 cm

The cat-tail shown in Photo 14 has leaves made with Formula 2.

NOTE: VERY SHORT PETALS
Many very short petals, such as those of hydrangea, are made on knitting needles. See projects and Formula 4, page 21, for details and instructions.

Formula 3: For Round Petals and Leaves

Big round petals or leaves, such as the leaves of the geranium and the African violet (Photo 15), are an exception to the rule. Formulas 1 and 2 are not applicable to this sort of leaf. To find the width of the stick for a round leaf, we first measure half the leaf. This becomes the width of the stick (RS).

For Formula 3 the length of loops on stick required = 3.5RS

Formula 2, For Short Leaves or Petals, from 1¼" (3 cm) up to 2" (5 cm)

In Formula 2 the length of loops required = 2RQ + 2RS

Formula 2 example: We need a petal ¾" (2 cm) wide and 1¾" (4.5 cm) long

RS = $^3/_8$" (1 cm) = the width of the stick

RQ = center of petal = S₁S₂ – 2RS

RQ in inches = 1¾" – 2 ($^3/_8$") = 1"

RQ in cm: 4.5 cm – 2 (1 cm) = 2.5 cm

Photo 15. African violets have round leaves made with Formula 3.

Formula 3 example: Let's say we need a round leaf 3" (8 cm) wide. The width of stick (or RS) is half the leaf = 1½" (4 cm). In this case, the length of loops on the stick should be:

in inches: 3.5 × 1½" = 5¼"

in cm: 3.5 × 4 cm = 14 cm

NOTE:
Please remember that we cannot give exact measurements since that depends on the tension of the wool we are working with and on the number of loops on the stick per inch or per cm. Person A will not produce the same result as Person B. The tauter we stretch the wool, the smaller the finished piece will be. It is therefore advisable for one person to make all the flower petals of the same flower, rather than two different persons.

Formula 4: For Very Narrow Leaves and Petals, and Very Small Petals

For extremely narrow leaves and petals, we use a knitting needle instead of a stick (see knitting needle method, page 14). The leaves of the gum tree (Photo 16) were made with Formula 4 and a knitting needle.

For Formula 4: The length of loops required on the stick = 2× length of petal or leaf.

Formula 4 example: If you need a petal 1" (2.5 cm) long, put a length of loops on the needle of 2" (5 cm).

It is advisable to make a sample chart of the finished petals or leaves with the corresponding needle number and the length of loops noted beside it for future use.

Photo 16. The long, narrow leaves of the gum tree were made using Formula 4.

How to Make Petals and Leaves with Smooth Edges

- Use thin florist wire for flower petals and thicker wire for the leaves, except when the flower petals are very long or very large, in which case use the heavier wire for the petals as well.
- Put the desired number of loops on the stick using the smooth-edge method. Bend the ends of the florist wire a little upwards to prevent the loops from falling off the wire when you slide them off the stick (Fig. 1-8a).

- Slide them off the stick (Fig. 1-8b). Bend the wire farther, until it is bent completely in half, and pinch it together (Fig. 1-8c). Wind the wires at point C with wool to a distance equal to the width of the stick (Fig. 1-8d).
- Pull the bottom edges at A and B to point D, hold them in position with thumb and forefinger, and tie them together with wool around the wires. Wind the wool downwards around the rest of the wire as needed (Fig. 1-8e).

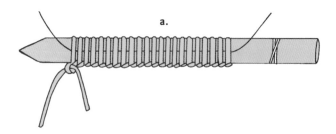

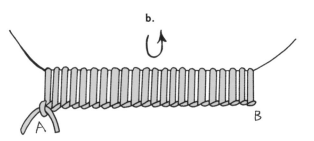

1-8. Making a smooth-edged petal or leaf. **a.** A length of loops has been cast on the stick; the ends of wire have been detached from the hook and from the rubber band, and wire has been bent up. **b.** The stitches are on wire with its ends bent up. **c.** Wire bent completely in half and pinched together, with braided edge of stitches on outside. **d.** Wool is wrapped around wire to a length equal to the width of the stick. **e.** Pull the ends of the petal or leaf down to D and tie them together with wool. Wind the wool down the rest of the wire, as needed.

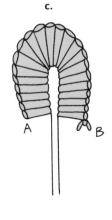

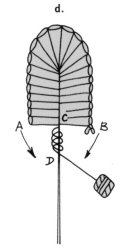

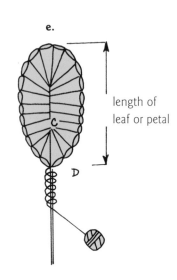

length of leaf or petal

- Dab the end of wool with UHU or other PVAc glue to prevent it from unwinding.

You can see three stages of a smooth edge leaf being formed in Photo 17.

How to Make Petals and Leaves with Frilled Edges

The process of making petals or leaves with curly or frilled edges is basically the same as making them with a smooth edge, but instead of using the smooth-edge method, we use the frilled-edge method of putting loops on the stick, leaving a space between bunches of 3 loops. The assisting wool should be at least 10 times the length of loops you want on the stick in this method. Photo 18 shows some stitches on a stick for the frilled edge method and a resulting frilled edge leaf, shown schematically in Fig. 1-9.

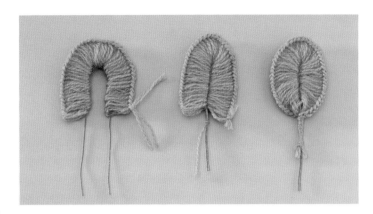

Photo 17. From left to right, a smooth-edge leaf being formed.

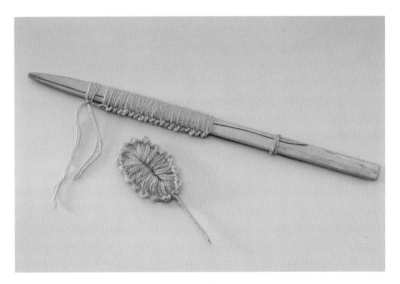

Photo 18. Loops on a stick for the frilled-edge method, which leaves a space between groups of 3 loops. On table, a resulting frilled-edge leaf.

1-9. Diagram of a petal or leaf with a frilled edge.

How to Make Round Petals or Leaves

- Make a length of loops on the stick as calculated in Formula 3 or listed in the project.
- To make an extra large round leaf, we need two rather sturdy florist wires, one for the stem and one for supporting the edge of the leaf, so it will stand out from its stem (Fig. 1-10a).
- After casting on the loops, slide the loops on their wire or wires off the stick.
- Slide the loops together in the center of the wire.

- Then pinch the wire in two, so that the loops fan out to form a circle. The bent wire becomes the stem of the leaf. If there are 2 wires, pinch together the one on the opposite side from the braided edge (Fig. 1-10b).
- Wind directly below where the end loops come together near the wire with green wool.
- Dot the end of wool with PVAc glue such as UHU to prevent the wool from unwinding.

Photo 19 shows the top and underside of a round leaf.

1-10. Making a large round leaf. **a.** Stitches cast on with 2 sturdy florist wires on the stick, one for the stem (A) and one for supporting the leaf edge (B). **b.** The finished leaf.

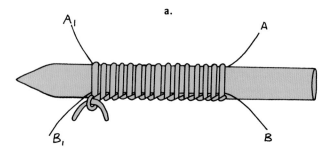
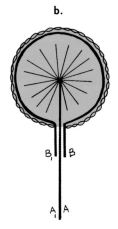

Photo 19. The top (left) and underside of a round leaf.

How to Make a Closed Bud

- Wind wool a number of times around cardboard that is 2⅜" (6 cm) wide (or as described in project notes); next cut both ends of the wool with scissors to make strands (Fig. 1-11a). For smaller buds, reduce the width of the cardboard.
- Dab the tip of a wire with PVAc glue, and distribute the wool strands evenly around the glued tip. Tie the strands together with sewing thread of the same color as the bud, positioning the strands at the tip of the wire so that only about ½" (1.3 cm) of the wool strands' length extends below the thread binding (Fig. 1-11b). Be sure the thread binding extends to the very tip of the wire.
- Pull the wool strands downwards all around the wire without exposing its tip, and bind them again with thread. With scissors, trim the strands that extend below the binding (Fig. 1-11c).
- Wrap binding and stem with green florist tape (Fig. 1-11d) to show less bulk at the calyx and so give it an all-in-one appearance. With the same color wool as the leaves, wind a calyx and stem from wool (Fig. 1-11e) below the bud. Photo 20 shows the bud-making process also.

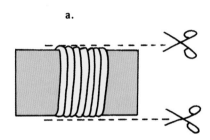

a.

1-11. Making a closed bud. **a.** Wrap wool around a cardboard 2⅜" (6 cm) wide and cut along both edges of cardboard to make strands. **b.** Dab tip of wire with glue, distribute wool strands around wire end, and wrap with thread. **c.** After pulling the loose ends of the wool strands down all around the wire end, tie the strands around the wire with thread again, at the correct length to make the bud. Then trim off any excess of strands that extend below the thread binding. **d.** Wrap the binding with florist tape. **e.** Wrap the binding with wool.

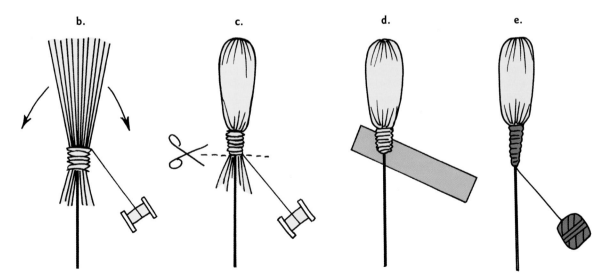

b.   c.   d.   e.

Photo 20. Steps (left to right) in making a closed buds: Winding wool on a cardboard, tying the wool strands to a wire, pulling down the strands of wool and tying them in place around the stem, wrapping 2 buds with florist tape (at right).

NOTE: SEPARATE CALYX
- Some buds have a separate calyx, added after the bud is created. See pages 30 to 34 for further information. Individual projects will specify which kind of calyx to make.

How to Extend a Too-Short Stem
- Extending a too-short stem requires special attention. When not properly done, it can cause much annoyance and ruin your work.
- Always tip the ends of wire with a dab of PVAc glue before binding them together firmly with sewing thread. Soften the bulges of the joint with a small strip of florist tape (Fig. 1-12a).
- Continue winding around the stem with wool (Fig. 1-12b). Dab PVAc at the end of the wool to prevent it from unwinding.

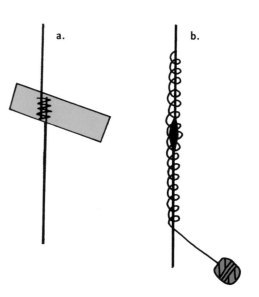

1-12. Extending a stem that is too short. **a.** Ends of two wires, dabbed in glue, are bound together firmly with sewing thread, The joint is wrapped with florist tape. **b.** The whole unit is wound with wool as usual.

How to Attach Leaves to a Stem

Attaching the leaves to the stem may be done without extending a wire in some cases. Leaves can be added directly by winding wool around the stem of the leaf and the flower stem in one continuous operation (Fig. 1-13). First bind each leaf in its proper place with thread. At the end of the stem, finish off with a dab of PVAc glue to prevent the wool from unwinding. However, leaves, buds, and flowers frequently are created on thin individual stems and then are attached to a thicker stem wire by tieing with thread, taping with florist tape, and binding with wool. See below for details.

The Process of Making Flowers in General

Here's a general overview of how to make a flower. See individual projects for specifics; not all flowers are made the same way.

Attaching the Stamens

The center of a flower consists in most cases of stamens. In flower-making, it's vital to make sure that the stamens stay securely on the stem. Always put a dab of PVAc glue at the base of the stamens before connecting them to the stem. The way you bind the stamens to the flower stem is the most important single operation in flower-making. Figure 1-14 will show you how.

- Take a number of ready-made stamens and bend them in half with the aid of thin, short florist wire (Fig. 1-14a). Make a few twists of the wires around themselves to secure. Bend the stamen ends upward.
- Lay the top of the wire that will become the flower stem at the same height as the twisted florist wire. Add a dab of PVAc glue and bind everything together with sewing thread (Fig. 1-14b); then add florist tape around the binding (Fig. 1-14c).

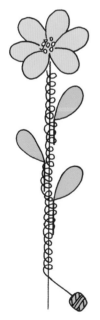

1-13. Attaching leaves to a stem. Each leaf, on its short stem, is bound into the central stem by the yarn wound around the stem.

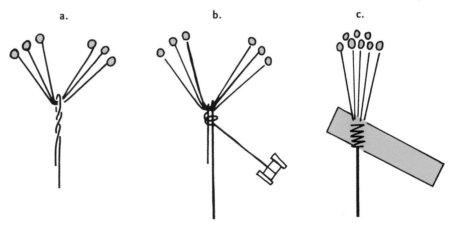

1-14. Attaching ready-made stamens to a wire. **a.** Twist wire around folded stamens. **b.** Bind stamens to top of stem wire with sewing thread, after adding a dab of glue. **c.** Wrap binding area only with florist tape and then with wool the color of the flower petals.

Attaching Petals and Leaves

In most cases, each petal and leaf is made separately on its own florist wire. Then they are joined together.

FOR FLOWERS WITH ONLY ONE LAYER OF PETALS

- After attaching stamens to the florist wire flower stem (see above and Figs. 1-14a through c), attach the petals one by one around the stamens.
- Bind the petals to the flower stem with thread (Fig. 1-15a); then wrap the entire stem with florist tape.
- Wind around the bindings of the petals on the stem with wool of the same color as the flower petals.
- Follow the project instructions to add a separate calyx, if necessary, to the flower. Otherwise wrap the stem wires below the petals with green wool to suggest a calyx.
- Wind downwards from the calyx with green wool, until you reach the place

for the first leaf. Add leaves as noted in the assembly instructions.
- Follow the project instructions to make groups of flowers if needed.

FOR FLOWERS WITH MORE THAN ONE LAYER OF PETALS

For flowers with many layers of petals, such as sunflower and chrysanthemum, we have to link the petals together before wrapping them around the flower center.

- Attach stamens if needed (refer to Fig. 1-14); follow individual project instructions for this.
- Link the petals of the first layer with two pieces of florist wire (Fig. 1-15b).
- Bind the petals around the stamens of the flower by twisting the ends of the wires together.
- In the same way, link and place the petals of the second layer with florist wire. Attach them beneath the first layer of petals on the stem. Move each

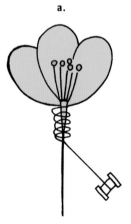

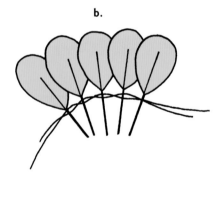

1-15. Attaching petals to a flower. **a.** For a simple flower, attach the petals one by one around the stamens by first binding with thread and then with wool. **b.** Bind the petals of many-petaled flowers, such as sunflower and chrysanthemum, using two strands of florist wire, before attaching the petals to the flower.

layer slightly around the stem to rotate it, so that the petals no longer fall exactly below those of the previous layer.

- Link the petals of the third layer and so on, until all layers are in their place. Photo 21 shows some decorative chrysanthemums, made with layers of petals.
- Attach the calyx and proceed as described above for flowers with one layer of petals.

FOR FLOWERS WITH SEVERAL LAYERS OF BRACTS

There are flowers with bracts, which are petal-like leaves. To attach them, follow the same procedure as for flowers with more than one layer of petals. Some examples of flowers with bracts are: cushion spurge (Photo 22), poinsettia, and waratah (fire bush).

Photo 21. These decorative chrysanthemums were made with several layers of petals.

Photo 22. Cushion spurge has flowers made with several layers of yellow-green bracts.

How to Make a Calyx

The calyx is a ring of leaflike structures called sepals, forming the outer support underneath a flower or bud. Calyxes are usually the same color as the leaves. Originally the calyx was closed around the bud to protect it. Some buds we make will have separate calyxes that we need to add. This will be noted in the projects. There are different kinds of calyxes: the closed calyx; the frilled calyx 1 and 2; the leafed calyx.

The Closed Calyx

- The closed calyx is added after a flower or bud is already attached to the stem.

- Use a stick ⅜" (1 cm) wide and the smooth-edge method (see page 10), with wool holding the stitches instead of a wire.
- Measure the girth (circumference) of the tied-on flower petals or bud with a strand of thread. Put a number of loops of green wool (or whatever color your calyx is) on the stick until its length on the stick equals the length of thread.
- Thread a yarn needle with wool and run the wool under the loops (Fig. 1-16a).
- Tie off the ends of the working and assisting wools.

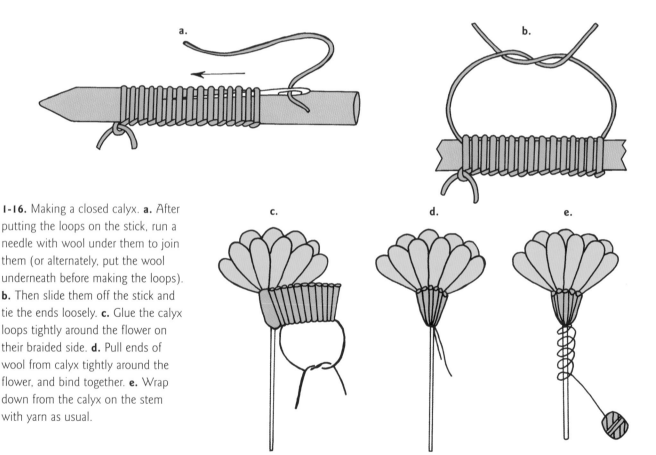

1-16. Making a closed calyx. **a.** After putting the loops on the stick, run a needle with wool under them to join them (or alternately, put the wool underneath before making the loops). **b.** Then slide them off the stick and tie the ends loosely. **c.** Glue the calyx loops tightly around the flower on their braided side. **d.** Pull ends of wool from calyx tightly around the flower, and bind together. **e.** Wrap down from the calyx on the stem with yarn as usual.

- Optional: You could fasten a length of green wool to the length of the stick before you start putting on the loops, as you did with a wire. This will save you from having to run a needle with wool under the loops later.
- While the loops are still on the stick, tie the ends of the long strand of wool loosely together (Fig. 1-16b).
- Slide all the loops on their wool strand from the stick.
- With PVAc glue, glue the loops of the calyx on their braided side a little above the binding of the flower (Fig. 1-16c). Let the glue dry.
- Next untie the loosely tied strand of wool holding the calyx and pull it taut around the stem (Fig. 1-16d) so the calyx is pulled all around the stem. Bind the ends of the wool firmly together. Continue winding the wool down the stem as usual (Fig. 1-16e) below the calyx. Photos 23 and 24 are examples of a bud and a flower with a closed calyx.

Photo 23. Closed calyx on a bud.

Photo 24. Closed calyx on a flower.

The Frilled Calyx, Method A

- Calyxes of flowers or buds usually consist of an uneven number of sepals, for instance 5, 7, 9.
- The petals or bud should already be in place on the stem wire.
- Check the individual project to learn how many strands of wool to work with for the calyx.
- Put a length of clear cellophane tape on the table with the sticky side up. Make upright waves of wool and press the wool strands firmly onto the tape as illustrated in Fig. 1-17a.

- Wrap the clear tape holding the wool strands around the base of the flower petals or bud (Fig. 1-17b), and then wind the stem with green wool as usual (Fig. 1-17c). Photo 25 shows frilled calyxes on buds.
- Sometimes the loops of a frilled calyx are then cut open to form fringe, as shown in the photo of dahlias (Photo 26). See project instructions for this information.

a.

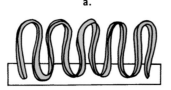

b.   **c.**

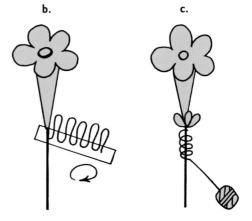

1-17. Making a frilled calyx, Method A.
a. Pressing strands of wool into a piece of cellophane tape at intervals. **b.** Wrapping the tape with wool around the base of the flower. **c.** Wrapping down the stem with wool below the calyx.

Photo 25. Frilled calyxes on buds.

Photo 26. Dahlias have a cut frilled calyx made by Method A.

The Frilled Calyx, Method B

- Here's another way to make a frilled calyx. Make the Method B frilled calyx after the flower petals or bud is attached to the stem.
- Use the smooth-edge method of casting on stitches, but don't use a wire or yarn support on the stick. Make a number of loops on the ¾" (2 cm) wide stick until you have about 2⅜" (6 cm) of loops. (Follow project directions if another size is called for.)

- Slide all the loops carefully off the stick. Do not pull!
- Put the flower face-down on the table. Spread an amount of PVAc glue right around the stem on the underside of the flower petals.
- Press the loops firmly onto the glue, circling around the stem until all are used up (Fig. 1-18a). Let the flower stay overnight to settle and dry.
- Turn right-side up (Fig. 1-18b). The asters shown in Photo 27 have calyxes made this way.

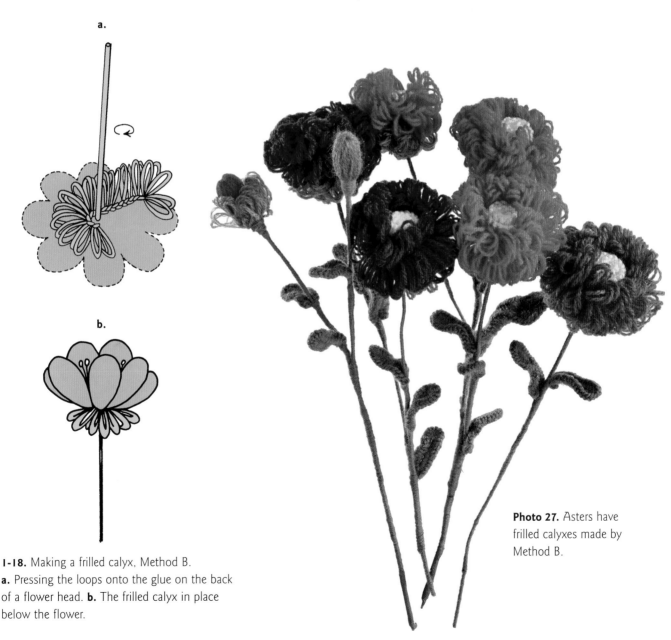

1-18. Making a frilled calyx, Method B.
a. Pressing the loops onto the glue on the back of a flower head. **b.** The frilled calyx in place below the flower.

Photo 27. Asters have frilled calyxes made by Method B.

The Leafed Calyx

- The leafed calyx usually consists of 5 sepals. Each sepal is like a little leaf. It is made on a knitting needle of US size 10 (UK 4, 6 mm) with a wire attached to its length (see Fig. 1-5).
- First we make 2 big sepals, A and B, one at a time:

  For sepal A: Cast on 40 loops on the knitting needle

  For sepal B: Cast on 60 loops on the knitting needle
- For each big sepal, tie together the ends of the assisting and working wool, having cut the latter off the ball, leaving a tail of wool.
- Release the wire ends and slide the loops, still on their wire, off the needle.
- Twist the wire ends of each big sepal A together as shown at the left of Fig. 1-19a.

- Next, divide big sepal A into 2 little sepals by binding it in 2 equal parts with thread (see right of Fig. 1-19a).
- In the same way, divide big sepal B into 3 little sepals (see Fig. 1-19b).
- By using sepals A + B we get 2 + 3 little sepals: a 5-leafed calyx.
- Place the sepals around the flower stem and bind them to the flower and stem with yarn to finish the leafed calyx (Fig. 1-19c). Photo 28 shows a leafed calyx.

NOTE: 2- OR 3-SEPAL CALYX

Sometimes we need only a 2-sepal calyx or a 3-sepal calyx. In that case, make the big sepal A for a 2-sepal calyx or the big sepal B for a 3-sepal calyx.

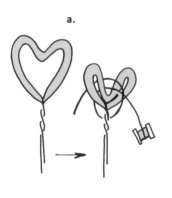

a.

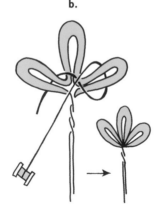

b.

c.

1-19. Making a leafed calyx with many sepals. **a.** Making two sepals out of one leaf. **b.** Making three sepals out of another leaf. **c.** Binding the leafed calyx to the flower with wool.

Photo 28. Leafed calyx on a crested gentian.

How to Make Berries

Making a round berry is very similar to making a closed bud (see Fig. 1-11).

- Wind wool a number of times around a cardboard about 2⅜" (6 cm) wide and cut the wool at both sides with scissors to make the short strands.
- Dab the tip of a wire for the stem with PVAc glue and arrange the wool strands around it, with most of the length of the strands extending up from the tip of the stem and about ½" (1 cm) extending below the tip. Tie the strands firmly together around the stem with sewing thread of the same color as the berry.
- Fray the wool of the berry with a special steel brush (available at craft stores) or with a stiff toothbrush until very fluffy and smooth.
- Pull the fluffy wool downwards as in the closed bud. Bind wool strand ends to stem; trim off excess wool ends below binding.
- Use the wispy remnants from the brush as stuffing to make the berry round and full.
- Wrap binding and stem as for a closed bud (see page 25). Photo 29 shows some pernettya berries made this way.

Photo 29. Pernettya berries.

How to Make Pompoms

Pompom Method A

- Use a pencil for a stick instead of a knitting needle. Instead of having the wire on the stick, secure a strand of wool along the length of the pencil with rubber bands.
- Wind another piece of wool around the pencil a number of times.
- Unfasten the two ends of the wool strand on the length of the pencil and tie them together in a knot (Fig. 1-20a).
- Slide the whole thing from the pencil. Tighten the knot to make a little pompom (Fig. 1-20b).
- One example of pompom use can be seen in Photo 30.

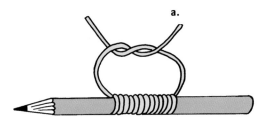

1-20. Making Pompom A. **a.** A length of wool, previously secured to the pencil, is used to tie together the loops on the pencil. **b.** The finished pompom.

Photo 30. The cosmos has flower centers of pompoms made by method A.

Pompom Method B

- To make pompoms by Method B, make a bundle of wool strands by wrapping wool around a cardboard about 3⅛" (8 cm) wide. Cut the wrapped strands into lengths of wool at both sides of the cardboard.
- Pinch the bundle of wool at two places with florist wire and twist the wire tight (Fig. 1-21a).
- Cut the wool with scissors in the middle of the two bundles to separate the pompoms. You can see one separated pompom in Fig. 1-21b.
- Fray the wool until very fluffy with a steel brush or a stiff toothbrush.
- Attach the pompom to the stem with yarn (Fig. 1-21c).
- Trim with scissors all around, until it is perfectly spherical (Fig. 1-21d).

Photo 31 shows the steps in making Pompom B.

Photo 31. Stages in making Pompom B.

a.

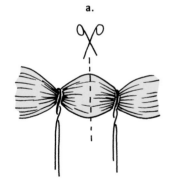

b.

c.

d.

1-21. Making Pompom B. **a.** A bundle of wool is pinched by two twisted wires and then cut apart into what will become two pompoms. **b.** One-half of the wool bundle. **c.** Attaching the pompom to the stem with wool. **d.** Trimmed pompom after it is fluffed out.

How to Make a Perfect Bow

You might want to add a decorative bow to your flower arrangement.

- For a simple ribbon bow, make two wide loops of ribbon and twist wire around the center of the loops to hold them in place.

- Then take a tail of the bow and run it around and through the upper wire loop to hide the join. Fig. 1-22a is the diagram; Fig. 1-22b shows the actual bow being formed.

- For a fuller bow, keep adding loops until the bow is a size you like (Figs. 1-22c and d).

a.

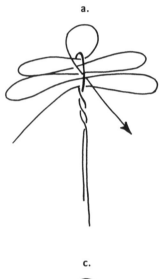

b.

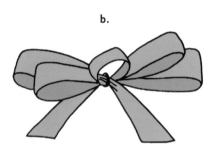

c.

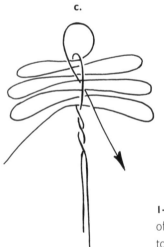

d.

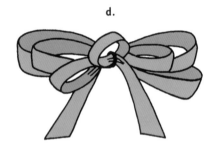

1-22. Making a perfect bow. **a.** Twist wire around two loops of ribbon in the center. **b.** Thread the ribbon back through the top of the wire. **c.** For a thicker bow, start with three loops of ribbon. Then thread the ribbon back through the top of the wire. **d.** The resulting bow.

The Flowers

Golden Ball Wattle
(Acacia podalyriifolia)

This native of Queensland and New South Wales, Australia, is a shrub or small evergreen tree. The fragrant flowers of the golden ball wattle resemble tiny yellow fluffy balls. It has silver-gray buds and leaves.

Tools: Stick ⅜" (1 cm) wide, toothbrush or steel brush, cardboard 3⅛" (8 cm) wide
Wool: Pale yellow, silver-gray
Other supplies: Florist wire, all-purpose galvanized wire, thread to match wool, PVAc glue

Closed Silver Bud
- Make a knot with 6 strands of 2-ply silver-gray wool for a closed bud.
- Attach each bud to a short length of florist wire by wrapping with silver-gray wool around wire (Fig. a). Dab the end of the wool with PVAc glue to prevent it from unwinding.

- Make 5 more buds in the same way.
- Attach the stems of the buds to each other on alternating sides by wrapping around both stems with silver-gray wool to form a stem with buds for the top of the branch (see Fig. b and photo).

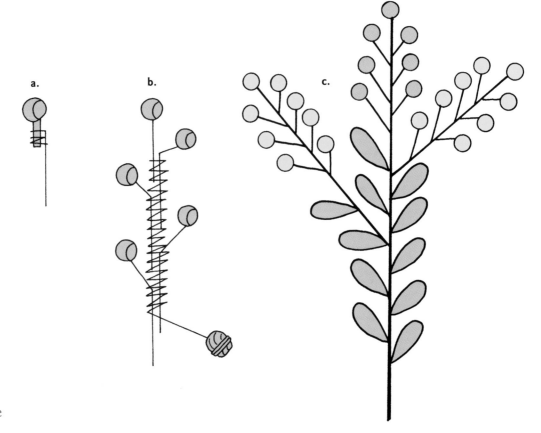

Golden ball wattle.
a. Attaching a bud to a stem with wool.
b. Five buds attached to each other on alternating sides with wool. **c.** The finished golden ball wattle.

Flower (Yellow Pompom)

- Wrap pale yellow wool around a cardboard 3⅛" (8 cm) wide and cut at both edges of the cardboard so you have strands in a bunch.
- Pinch the bundle of pale yellow wool in 2 places with 2 pieces of florist wire and twist them tight (see method of Pompom B, page 37, Fig. 1-21).
- Cut the bundle into 2 parts to make two pompoms.
- Fray the wool of the pompoms until very fluffy with a steel brush or a stiff toothbrush.
- Trim with scissors all around until each is perfectly spherical.
- Prepare 7 to 8 pompoms for each side stem (see photo).

Leaf

Color: Silver-gray. Method: Formula 2, smooth edge, using a stick ⅜" (1 cm) wide. Length of loops on stick: 2¾" (7 cm). Length of leaf: 1¾" (4.5 cm). Prepare a number of leaves (see photo).

Assembly

- Attach pompoms to each other in the same manner as you did for the buds, on alternating sides, using 7 or 8 yellow pompoms to make a side stem and wrapping the stem with silver-gray wool in between.
- For the main stem, bind the stem of silver buds on the top and attach the side stems on alternate sides of it, followed by more leaves (see Fig. c). Arrange the flowers and leaves as in the photo.

South African Lily

(*Agapanthus hybrid*)

The South African lily has 6-petaled flowers, clustered in an umbel radiating from the top of the stalk like a bursting firework.

Tools: Knitting needle US size 10 (UK size 4 or 6 mm), stick ⅝" (1.5 cm) wide, cardboard 2⅜" (6 cm) wide
Wool: Blue, dark green
Other supplies: Light blue ready-made stamens, stiff florist wire, florist tape, PVAc glue, sewing thread to match wool, round wooden stick, ⅜"(1 cm) wide and 15¾" (40 cm) long for stalk

The finished South African lily.

Flower Petal

Color: Blue. Number: 6 petals per flower. Method: Knitting needle method, Formula 4, with a US size 10 (UK size 4) knitting needle. Length of loops on the needle: 3½" (9 cm). Length of a petal: 1¾" (4.5 cm).

Flower Assembly

Bind 6 stamens on a florist wire. Attach the petals around the stamens, shaping as shown in photo. Bind the petals to the flower stem with dark green wool to suggest a calyx, and bind down the stem for a few inches with green wool. This completes one flower of the umbel.

Bud

Color: Blue. Method: See closed bud (Fig. 1-11). Length of bud: 1⅜" (3.5 cm). Make each bud on its own stem wire. Bind around the base of the bud with dark green wool to suggest a calyx.

Leaf

Color: Use 3 strands of dark green 2-ply wool and stiff florist wire. **Method:** Use Formula 1, smooth edge, with a stick ⅝" (1.5 cm) wide. Length of loops on stick: 10⅞" (27.5 cm). Length of leaf: 6⅜" (16 cm).

Main Stem

The stem is about ⅜" (1 cm) in diameter and about 15¾" (40 cm) long. For this stem, use a round wooden stick, wrapped with florist tape.

Assembly

- Attach buds and flowers in an umbel shape to the top of the stick that will become the stem (see photo and figure).
- After winding down the stem with green wool, attach the swordlike leaves near the bottom.

Cat-tail, Love-lies-bleeding

(*Amaranthus caudatus*)

The cat-tail is an annual with edible seeds, originally from India and South America. In many parts of the world amaranths are an important food source. It is a popular garden plant.

Tools: Knitting needle size US 10 (UK 4, or 6 mm), stick ⅝" (1.5 cm) wide
Wool: Dark red, moss green
Other supplies: Tissue paper, florist tape, thick florist wire, thick all-purpose wire or branch for main stem, PVAc glue, sewing thread to match wool

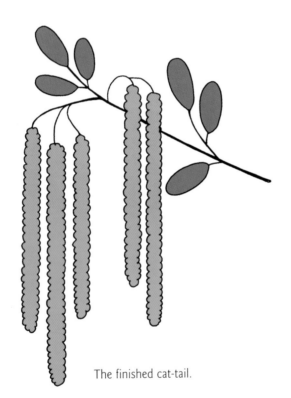

The finished cat-tail.

Flower

Color: Dark red (with 4 strands of 2-ply wool). Method: Knitting needle method without wire (smooth edge), on a needle size US 10 (UK 4, 6 mm). Length of cat-tail, 8" (20 cm).

- Prepare a few tissue-paper padded all-purpose wire stems about ³⁄₁₆" (0.5 cm) in diameter, and wrap with florist tape. You will need one for each hanging cat-tail.
- For each cat-tail, make enough loops on the knitting needle with dark red wool, without using a wire on the needle, to create a frill that will cover the desired length on the needle.
- Continue as in Fern (see page 90): Slide the flower loops from the knitting needle, little by little, while spiraling the loops around a tissue-paper-padded stem, but make the frills denser than

for the fern. Glue the ends of wool in place with a dab of PVAc.

- Wrap each cat-tail stem for 2" (5 cm) with green wool.

Leaf

Color: Moss green. Method: Formula 2, smooth edge, using a stick ⅝" (1.5 cm) wide. Length of loops on stick: 2¾" (7 cm). Length of leaf: 2" (5 cm). Wrap each leaf stem for 1" (2.5 cm) below the leaf with green wool.

Assembly

- Bind 2 or 3 leaves to the top end of a thick padded wire or stick for the main stem.
- Bind cat-tail stems together in groups of 2 with green wool for about 1" (2.5 cm).
- Continue to wrap down the main stem with green wool, joining the groups of flowers to it.
- Add more leaves below the flowers (see photo).

Snapdragon

(*Antirrhinum hybrid*)

Although these snapdragons look very intricate, they are actually very simple to make. Choose the same wool color for all the flowers and buds on a stalk; make several colors of snapdragon if you like.

Tools: Knitting needle size US 8 (UK 6, or 5 mm), stick ⅜" (1 cm) wide
Wool: Off white, orange, wine red, yellow (use one or more colors), green
Other supplies: PVAc glue, florist wire, florist tape, all-purpose galvanized wire, sewing thread to match wool

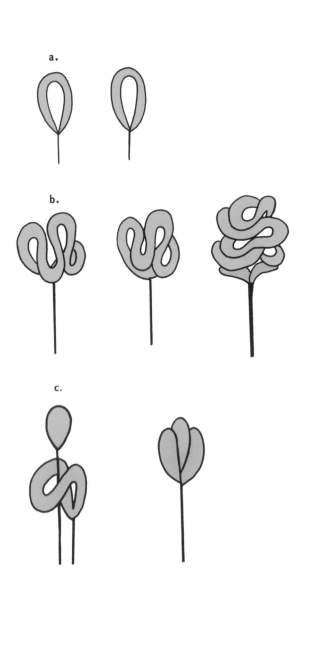

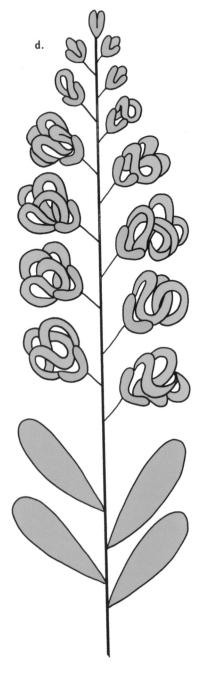

Snapdragon. **a.** Two petal parts are bent and combined to make an open flower (**b**), with a calyx added at the bottom (far right of b). **c.** To make an open bud, knot a triple strand of colored wool and then insert in the middle of a 2-sepal green calyx. **d.** Arrange flowers, buds, and leaves as shown.

Flowers

FULLY OPENED FLOWER

Color: Your choice for flower. Method: Knitting needle method, smooth edge; knitting needle size US 8 (UK 6). For each petal cast on 60 loops.

- After casting on loops, remove the wire along with loops from the knitting needle, and twist the 2 ends of the wire together (Fig. a). Make another petal the same way. Curl each petal and glue one curled petal on top of the other (Fig. b, center) to make a flower.
- Make a 5-sepal green calyx (see leafed calyx, Fig. 1-19) and bind the 5-sepal green calyx at the base of the flower petals.
- Wrap the stem wire a little way with green wool below the calyx.

HALF-OPEN FLOWER

Color: Match fully opened flower.
Method: Knitting needle method, smooth edge; knitting needle size, US 8 (UK 6, 5 mm). For each petal cast on 60 loops.

- After casting on loops, remove the wire along with loops from the knitting needle, and twist the 2 ends of the wire together to form a petal as in Fig. a.
- Curl the petal as you did for the fully opened flower.
- Make and place a 3-sepal green calyx at the base of the flower (see Fig. 1-19b for making a 3-leafed calyx).
- Wrap the stem wire a little way with green wool below the calyx.

Buds

PARTLY OPEN BUD

- Tie a knot of a triple strand of wool of the same color as the flower.
- Make a 2-sepal green calyx (see Fig. 1-19a) and insert the knot between the sepals (see Fig. c).
- Wrap the stem wire a little way with green wool.

CLOSED BUD

Make a closed bud that consists of only a 2-sepal green calyx (see Fig. 1-19a); it will go at the top of the main stem, above the partly open buds. Wrap down the bud's stem an inch (2.5 cm) with green wool.

Leaf

Color: Green. Method: Formula 1, smooth edge on a stick: ⅜" (1 cm) wide. Length of loops on stick: 6" (15 cm). Length of leaf: 3½" (9 cm).

Assembly

- Prepare many fully opened flowers, as well as some half-open flowers and buds of both kinds.
- Starting at the top of a wire with a closed bud, arrange the buds and flowers in an alternating pattern around the spike (main stem), binding them in place; see photo and Fig. d.
- Put the leaves a few inches (5 or 7 cm) down from the flowers on the main stem. They wrap right around the stem with no petiole (see photo).

New York Aster

(*Aster novi belgii*)

At one time, New York was called New Belgium, thus this flower's Latin name. Make a whole bunch of asters in colors of your choice. A basketful of asters can be made in a jiffy.

Tools: Stick ¾" (2 cm) wide, knitting needle US size 10 (UK size 4, or 6 mm), crochet hook
Wool: White, red, magenta, and purple for flowers (your choice); yellow, green
Other supplies: All-purpose galvanized wire, florist wire, florist tape, matching thread, PVAc glue, sewing thread to match wool, waxed paper

Calyx of Flower and Bud

Color: Green. Method: Smooth edge, without wire, on a stick ¾" (2 cm) wide. Length of loops on stick: 4" (10 cm). See frilled calyx, Method B, page 33. Make a calyx for each flower and bud.

Stamens (Flower Center)

Color: Yellow. Method: Chainstitch a 2" (5 cm) long yellow chain with the crochet hook, using double strands of yellow wool. It will be curled on itself and glued in place to become the flower center.

New York Aster. On left, bud with calyx.

Flower Petals

Color: Choose white, red, magenta, or purple. Method: Smooth edge, made without a wire, on a stick ¾" (2 cm) wide. Length of loops on stick: 11" (28 cm).

- Put a sheet of wax paper on the work table.
- Slide the loop section off the stick and let it curl freely onto itself in a circle. Spread a generous amount of PVAc glue onto the center of the loops; then press the curled loop section, glued side down, onto the sheet of waxed paper. Let it dry overnight. Then peel the dried flower petals off the waxed paper.
- Tip the end of a florist wire stem with PVAc glue and stab it through the center of the flower petals.
- Glue the flower center snailwise to the top center of the flower petals, and glue the frilled calyx B in a circle around the stem beneath the flower.

Buds

CLOSED BUD

Color: Green. Method: See closed bud (Fig. 1-11). Wrap the stem of the bud below its attachment to the florist wire with green wool to imitate a calyx (see photo).

OPEN BUD

Color: Match color of flower for bud shape. Method: See closed bud (Fig. 1-11). Glue a green frilled calyx B below the bud on the florist wire stem. Wrap beneath the frilled calyx with green wool, pushing the frilled calyx upwards so it surrounds the bud (see photo).

Leaves

SMALL LEAF

Color: Green. Method: Knitting needle, smooth edge, Formula 4. Knitting needle US size 10 (UK size 4, or 6 mm). Length of loops on needle: 2 (5 cm). Length of leaf: 1" (2.5 cm).

LARGE LEAF

Color: Green. Method: Knitting needle, smooth edge method, Formula 4, on a knitting needle size US 10 (UK 4, 6 mm). Length of loops on needle: 2⅜" (6 cm). Length of leaf: 3¼" (8 cm).

Assembly

- Wrap down each flower and bud stem with green wool, adding leaves as shown in photo and diagram.
- Join some bud stems together, and join some flower stems together partway down the stem, as shown in photo.

Bouvardia

(Bouvardia 'President Cleveland')

The bouvardia belongs to the unusual group of flowers that have an even number of flower petals. Bouvardia has small 4-petaled florets, grouped in small bunches like little posies. The posies are grouped as a compound umbel. The stick and the knitting needle we have used so far won't work for the bouvardia with its tiny flower petals. For this reason, we resort to another technique. Let's call it the thick yarn method, because the working material we use is not a few plies of thin yarn as usual, but the full unseparated rayon yarn that is about the weight of knitting worsted.

Tools: Sticks ⅜" (1 cm) and ⅝" (1.5 cm) wide, pencil
Wool: Fire-red unseparated yarn for flowers, 2-ply red and dark green wool
Other supplies: White ready-made stamens, PVAc glue, red sewing thread, florist wire, florist tape, all-purpose galvanized wire

Bouvardia. **a.** A bunch of 5 florets.
b. The finished bouvardia.

Floret and Floret Bunch

Color: Fire-red. Method: Thick yarn method.

- Tie a single stamen on a 2" (5 cm) long wire.
- Thread a needle with red thread. Take fire-red undivided yarn, wind it once around a pencil, and tie it with red sewing thread to be the first petal. Leave it on the pencil.
- Wind yarn around the pencil again; bind it with red sewing thread for the second petal, and so on, until there are 4 petals linked with thread on the pencil.
- Slide the petals off the pencil.
- Wrap the 4 petals around the stamen wire and bind them in place with thread to make a floret.
- Wind with thin red wool about 1⅜" (3.5 cm) down the wire and cut the wool.

- Make 5 of these little florets and bind them together as one little bunch.
- See below for calyx of bunch.

CALYX OF BUNCH
- Make a 3-sepal calyx from green wool (see leafed calyx, page 34, Fig. 1-19b). Attach the 3-sepal calyx to the base of each 5-floret bunch (see Fig. a and photo).

- Wind downwards on the bunch stem with green wool, and dab the wool with PVAc glue to prevent it from unwinding.

Leaves

LEAF A
Color: Dark green. Method: Formula 1, smooth edge, on a stick ⅜" (1 cm) wide. Length of loops on stick: 4" (10 cm). Length of leaf: 2½" (6.5 cm).

LEAF B
Color: Dark green. Method: Formula 1, smooth edge, on a stick ⅝" (1.5 cm) wide. Length of loops on stick: 4½" (11.5 cm). Length of leaf: 3⅛" (8 cm).

Assembly
Make side stems of leaves, starting with 2 of leaf A and binding down the stem with dark green wool, adding leaves opposite each other.
- Bind eight 5-floret groups together on a main stem to become a compound umbel (see Fig. b).
- Attach 2 small leaves a bit below the flowers and add larger leaves opposite each other, farther down the stem.
- Join the leaf stems to the main stem, adding a few more leaves.

Golden Shower Tree

(*Cassia fistula*)

The canary-yellow flowers of the golden shower tree are borne on drooping racemes 12" to 20" (30 to 60 cm) long. Each open flower has yellow filaments, which turn up at the ends like skis.

Tools: Sticks ⅜" (1 cm) and ¾" (2 cm) wide
Wool: Canary yellow, light yellow-green, dark green, brown
Other supplies: Yellow ready-made stamens, florist wire, thick all-purpose wire or a stick for main stem, PVAc glue, sewing thread to match yarns

Filaments of Flowers

To make filaments, wrap about 2⅜" (6 cm) florist wire with canary yellow wool. Bend double with the ends turned up like skis.

Flowers

FULLY OPENED FLOWER

Color: Canary yellow. Petals: 5 per flower. Method: Formula 2, smooth edge, on a stick ⅜" (1 cm) wide. Length of loops on stick: 2⅜" (6 cm). Length of petal: 1½" (4 cm).

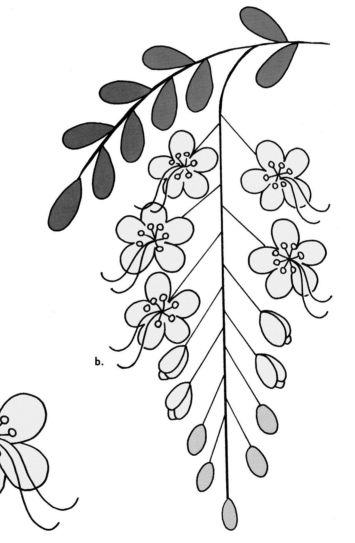

Golden shower tree. **a.** A fully opened flower with filaments and stamens. **b.** A branch of flowers and buds, and a joined leaf branch.

- To assemble a flower, bind the filaments and 6 stamens together on a florist wire stem and bind 5 petals around them (Fig. a).
- Wind a calyx with light yellow-green wool around stem below petals (see photo).

HALF-OPEN FLOWER

Color: Canary yellow. Number: 3 petals per flower. Method: Make petals as for fully opened flower.

- To assemble petals, bind the wires of the 3 petals together to make a stem. Pinch the 3 petals together at their tops.
- Wind a calyx of light yellow-green wool around stem (see photo).

Buds

Colors: Light yellow-green and canary yellow. Method: Closed bud method; see Fig. 1-11.

- Make tiny closed buds in light yellow-green. Make each bud on its own florist wire stem.
- Make some larger closed buds in canary yellow also, the same way.
- Wrap calyxes of buds in light yellow-green wool on stem below bud.

Leaf

Color: Green. Method: Formula 1, smooth edge, on a stick ¾" (2 cm) wide. Length of loops on stick: 4¾" (12 cm). Length of leaflet: 3¼" (8 cm).

- The compound leaves are made up of 7 leaflets, carried on separate side stems from the flowers (see Fig. b and photo).
- Make each leaflet on its own florist wire stalk.
- Join the leaflets on a side stem, starting with one leaf at the top and adding 3 pairs of leaves alternate to each other on the side stem (see photo).
- Make several leaf stems the same way.

Assembly of Flower Stem

- See Fig. b and photo. Attach a few small yellow-green buds at the end of each main flower stem, which will carry the flowers and buds.
- Add some yellow buds after that, winding down the stem with yellow-green wool in between.
- Attach some partially open flowers and then some open flowers to complete the hanging flower stem.

Assembly

- Wind a thick wire or stick with florist tape for a main stem.
- Follow photo to attach the flower stems and leaf stems to the main stem, wrapping main stem with brown wool.

Early Jessamine 'newellii'

(*Cestrum fasciculatum 'newellii'*)

Early jessamine 'newellii' has a compound umbel made of clusters of tubular flowers. It is a vigorous evergreen shrub, very popular with hummingbirds.

Tools: Knitting needle size US 10 (UK 4), stick ⅜" (1 cm) wide
Wool: Crimson, green
Other supplies: Florist wire, florist tape, PVAc glue, thread to match wool, thick all-purpose wire for main stem, clear cellophane tape

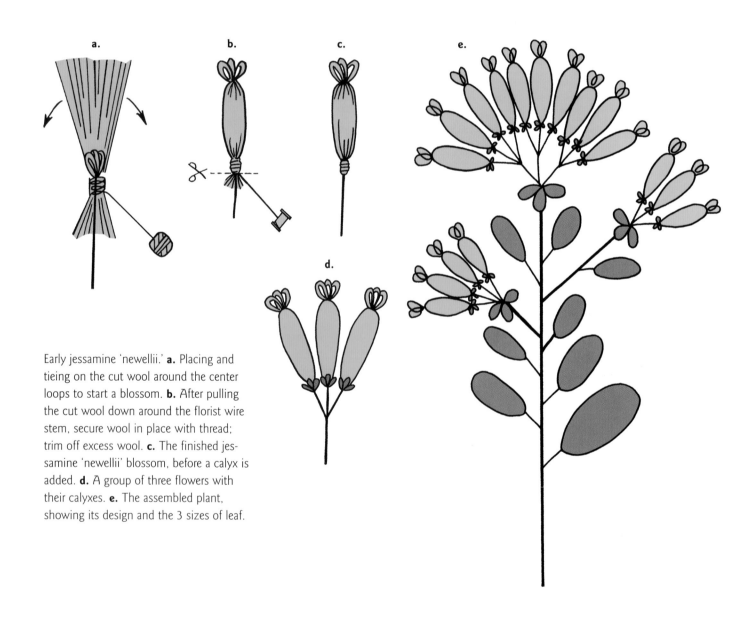

Early jessamine 'newellii.' **a.** Placing and tieing on the cut wool around the center loops to start a blossom. **b.** After pulling the cut wool down around the florist wire stem, secure wool in place with thread; trim off excess wool. **c.** The finished jessamine 'newellii' blossom, before a calyx is added. **d.** A group of three flowers with their calyxes. **e.** The assembled plant, showing its design and the 3 sizes of leaf.

Flower Body and Flower Assembly

Color: Crimson. Method: Tie 3 loops of wool together on a florist wire and continue as in making a closed bud, as shown here in Figs. a to c. See page 25, making a closed bud, and Fig. 1-11 for details.

- Cut strands of crimson wool and tie with crimson wool around the 3 loops you just added to the stem (Fig. a).
- Pull the strands down around the wire to make the tubular flower, and tie again with thread as shown in Fig. b. The three loops will appear at the top of the bud.
- Trim off the excess of wool strands below the tieing thread to complete the closed flower (Fig. c).
- Bind a frilled calyx under each flower (see below).
- Wind down the stem with dark green wool below the calyx a short way.

LEAF B (MEDIUM LEAF)

Color: Green. Method: Smooth edge, Formula 2. Stick: ⅜" (1 cm) wide. Length of loops on stick: 2⅜" (6 cm). Length of leaf: 1½" (4 cm). Wind down the wire below the leaf with green wool for a short way for a leaf stalk.

LEAF C (LARGE LEAF)

Color: Green. Method: Smooth edge, Formula 1. Stick: ⅜" (1 cm) wide. Length of loops on stick: 3½" (9 cm). Length of leaf: 2⅜" (6 cm). Wind down the wire below the leaf with green wool for a short way for a leaf stalk.

Assembly

- Make the compound umbel by first assembling groups of 3 or 4 tubular flowers.
- Add small leaves (leaf A) below where the assembled flower stems come together.
- Add a few of leaf B farther down the flower stem.
- Then join the assembled stems to the main stem as shown (Fig. e and photo), adding leaves as shown, with the larger leaves near the bottom of the stem.

Frilled Calyx

Color: Green. Make a calyx of 3 looped sepals for each flower. Method: See frilled calyx, Method A, page 32 (Fig. 1-17a).

Leaves

LEAF A (SMALL LEAF)

Color: Green. Method: Smooth edge, knitting needle, size US 10 (UK 4, 6 mm). Length of loops on needle: 1½" (4 cm). Length of leaf: 1" (2.5 cm). Wind down the wire below the leaf with green wool for a short way for a leaf stalk.

Corydalis

(*Corydalis cashmeriana*)

The corydalis has flowers that look like perching blue birds. The flowers consist of 2 petals around a dark blue center at the front of the tubular body that ends in a tail.

Tools: Knitting needles, US sizes 10½ and 10 (UK sizes 3 and 4, or 6.5 and 6 mm), stick ⅜" (1 cm) wide
Wool: Light blue, dark blue, olive green
Other supplies: Florist wire, thick all-purpose wire for stem, florist tape, PVAc glue, sewing threads to match wool

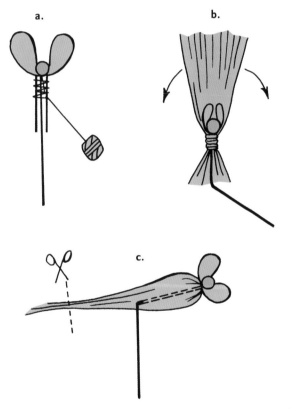

Corydalis. **a.** Center of flower, tieing 2 petals around the stamen. **b.** The center is wrapped with light blue wool strands like the start of a closed bud or early jessamine 'newellii'; then the strands are pulled down and glued into a tail. **c.** Trimming the tail. **d.** The finished corydalis.

Flower Petal

Color: Light blue. Number: 2 per flower. Method: Knitting needle method, Formula 4, smooth edge. Knitting needle size US 10½ (UK 3). Length of loops on needle: 1½" (4 cm). Length of petal: ¾" (2 cm).

Stamen

Color: Dark blue. Method: Make a knot out of 3 short strands of wool for the stamen.

Flower Body and Flower Assembly

Color: Light blue. Method: Flower body is modified from early jessamine 'newellii':

- Tie the stamen to a 4" (10 cm) florist wire flower stem and tie 2 petals around the center (see Fig. a).
- Then cut strands of light blue wool, as for a closed bud, and tie them around the stamen and petals as shown in Fig. b. Most of the length of the strands extends above the wire.
- Pull the wool strands down all around the center. However, do not bind the wool strands a second time as you do for early jessamine 'newellii.' Instead, see Fig. c and bend the flower stem wire at almost a right angle downwards and glue the strands together with dabs of PVAc glue, layer after layer,

shaping them into a tail. Be careful not to let the glue seep through the outer layer of wool.

- Next, trim the tail with scissors. At the end of the tail, glue and wrap a few turns of light blue wool.
- Wrap down the florist wire stem with olive green wool for a few inches (7.5 cm).

Calyx

Color: Olive green. Method: Knitting needle method, Formula 4, smooth edge, using knitting needle size US 10 (UK 4, or 6 mm). Length of loops on needle: 5½" (12 cm). Length of calyx: 2⅜" (6 cm). Make about 10 calyx parts, which look like long thin green leaves, for a group of blossoms.

Leaf

Color: Olive green. Method: Formula 2, frilled edge, on a stick ⅜" (1 cm) wide. Length of loops on stick: 2" (5 cm). Length of leaf: 1⅜" (3.5 cm). Make 7 or more leaves for each main stem. Join the leaves in groups of 3 on side stems (see photo), and shape each leaf into 3 lobes, as shown in photo. Make a few leaves with only two lobes each, to attach directly onto main stem.

Assembly

- Attach some of the blossoms on their bent stems in a whorl around the top of a thick wire main stem, with the blossom openings facing outward.
- Attach some of the calyx sections in a whorl at the top of the main stem, bent upwards.
- Attach more blossoms in a whorl just below the calyx sections, and then add more calyx parts. Bend these calyx parts outwards as shown in photo.
- Wrap down the stem with green wool and attach a few double-lobed leaves directly to main stem; then bind in the groups of 3 leaves on their side stems, as shown in photo.

Cosmos

(*Cosmos bipinnatus*)

This cosmos is an annual that has red, white, pink, or purple flowers. It is native to Mexico and the southwestern United States. Cosmos are good for attracting butterflies.

Tools: Stick ⅝" (1.5 cm) wide, cardboard 1¼" (3 cm) wide
Wool: Soft rose, light green, yellow
Other supplies: Florist wire, florist tape, PVAc glue, sewing thread to match the wool colors

Stamen

Color: Yellow. Method: See Pompom A, page 36 (Fig. 1-20). Make one pompom stamen for each flower.

Flowers

OPEN FLOWER

Color: Soft rose; 5 petals per flower.
Method: Formula 2, frilled edge, on a stick ⅝" (1.5 cm) wide. Length of loops on stick: 2¾" (7 cm). Length of petal: 2" (5 cm).

- Arrange and bind the petals on a florist wire stem so they overlap slightly to form a circular flower.
- Glue a yellow stamen in the middle of the flower; see photo.
- Wind down the stem below the petals with green wool to suggest a calyx and cover the stem.

Cosmos, showing arrangement of closed buds (top), half-open flower (left), open flowers, and leaves on stem.

HALF-OPEN FLOWER

Color: Soft rose. Method: Same as
for open flower petals, but make
1 petal per half-open flower. To
make a half-open flower, roll the
petal; then wind stem with green
wool below it to suggest a calyx.

Closed Bud

Color: Green. Method: See closed bud,
page 25, but use 1¼" (3 cm) wide
cardboard; see Fig. 1-11 for reference.

Leaves

Color: Green. Method: See the leaves
of the heath (page 77).

Assembly

Arrange buds, flowers, and leaves
as shown in the figure and
the photo. Start with closed
buds and leaves, and wrap
leaves into green wool
that goes around stems.

Lantern Tree

(*Crinodendron hookeranum*)

The lantern tree looks like a Christmas tree full of bright red hanging lanterns. It can grow very tall.

Tools: Sticks ⅜" (1 cm) and ⅝" (1.5 cm) wide, knitting needle size US 10 (UK 4, or 6 mm)
Wool: Bright red, moss green, dark green
Other supplies: Florist wire, stick about ¼" (5 mm) in diameter for main stem, florist tape, sewing thread to match wool, PVAc glue

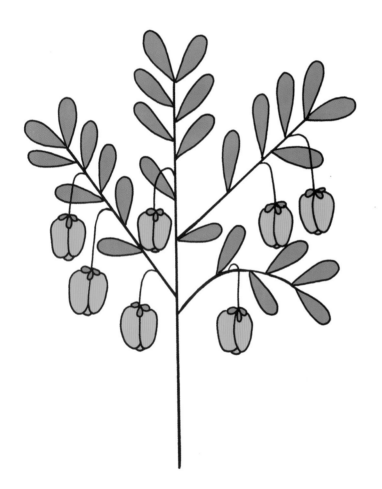

The finished lantern tree.

Flower Petal

Color: Bright red. Number: 4 per flower. Method: Formula 1, smooth edge, on a stick ⅝" (1.5 cm) wide. Length of loops on stick: 4½" (11.5 cm). Length of petal: 3⅛" (8 cm).

Calyx

Color: Moss green. Method: See leafed calyx, Fig. 1-19, and make a 5-sepal leafed calyx on a US size 10 (UK size 4, 6 mm) knitting needle. Number of loops on needle = 40 loops for half the calyx. Repeat again for 2nd half: make half the calyx out of each group of 60 loops. Make a calyx for each flower and bud.

Bud

Color: Bright red. Method: Like petals, using a stick the same size. Length of loops on stick: 2½" (6.5 cm). Length of petal: 1½" (3.5 cm).

Leaf

Color: Moss green. Method: Formula 1, smooth edge, on a stick ⅜" (1 cm) wide. Length of loops on stick: 4¾" (12 cm). Length of leaf: 3" (7.5 cm).

Side Stem without Flowers

Color: Dark green. For side stem without flowers, make a small side branch as for the blood-twig dogwood (see page 73), but with green wool (lower right in photo). Attach a leaf near the join.

Assembly

- Refer to photo and drawing. Attach the leaves in opposite pairs to a side stem with dark green wool. Curve leaves as shown.
- Shape each flower in an upside-down bowl form and add a 5-sepal leafed calyx to each.
- Attach flowers so they hang, as illustrated, interspersed with leaves, on the side stems and on the main stem.
- Hang buds and their calyxes in the same way.
- Attach the extra side stem without flowers below other stems.

Tulip

(Darwin tulipa)

Tulips occur in an wide array of colors, so you can make them in almost any color imaginable.

Tools: Stick ⅝" (1.5 cm) wide
Wool: Yellow, orange, red, green, black
Other supplies: Florist wire, heavy all-purpose galvanized wire, florist tape, green tissue paper, PVAc glue, sewing threads to match wool

Flower Petal

Color: Yellow, orange, or red. **Number:** 5 petals per flower. **Method:** Formula 1, smooth edge, on a stick ⅝" (1.5 cm) wide. Length of loops on stick: 4½" (11.5 cm). Length of petal: 3⅛" (8 cm).

Stamen

Color: Black. **Number:** 3 stamens per flower. **Method:** Use wire wrapped with black wool (see the spoon shapes of the blood-twig dogwood, page 73).

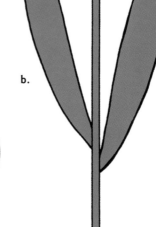

a.   **b.**

Tulip. **a.** Three stamens attached to a stem, with the first two petals around them. **b.** The finished tulip, with leaves attached.

Leaf

Color: Green. Method: Formula 1, smooth edge, on a stick ⅝" (1.5 cm) wide. Use a stiff florist wire and 3 strands of wool. Length of loops on stick: 11" (27.5 cm). Length of leaf: 6½" (16 cm).

Assembly

- The tulip has a thick stem, but we don't need a stick. Heavy all-purpose wire wrapped with tissue paper is sufficient. Please remember, always wrap with florist tape first, before winding the stem with wool.
- Attach 3 stamens to the main stem and group the 5 petals around it, cupping them like a bowl (Fig. a).
- Wrap down the stem with green wool and attach the straight leaves farther down the stem (Fig. b).

Decorative Chrysanthemum

(Dendranthema grandiflorum)

The chrysanthemum is a member of the same family as the daisy. It has a large flower head made of many small florets, although we usually call them "petals." Chrysanthemums come in many different colors.

Tools: Knitting needle size US 10 (UK 4, or 6 mm), stick ⅜" (1 cm) wide
Wool: Lemon yellow, dark green
Other supplies: Florist wire, thick all-purpose wire for main stem, florist tape, PVAc glue, sewing thread to match wool

Flower Petals

PETAL A
Color: Lemon yellow. **Number:** 27 petals per flower. **Method:** Knitting needle, Formula 4, smooth edge; needle size US 10 (UK 4, or 6 mm). Length of loops on needle: 3¾" (9.5 cm). Length of petal: 2³⁄₁₆" (5.5 cm).

PETAL B
Color: Lemon yellow. **Number:** 38 petals per flower. **Method:** Knitting needle, Formula 4, smooth edge, needle size US 10 (UK 4, or 6 mm). Length of loops on needle: 4⅛" (10.5 cm). Length of petal: 2⅜" (6 cm).

Flower Center

Wind a florist wire about 1½" (4 cm) down with a double strand of yellow wool (Fig. a) and bend the wrapped section double (Fig. b). This will become the center of the flower.

Bud

- Make a knot with 4 strands of yellow wool.
- Make a dark green closed calyx for the bud (see closed calyx, Fig. 1-16), and put the calyx around the knot. The closed bud is shown in Fig. g.

Flower Assembly

- The chrysanthemum flower consists of 5 layers of petals. Before starting to attach the petals to the stem, pinch each petal double with thumb and forefinger, at the same time bending it slightly backwards (see Fig. c). The braided side of the petal should face outwards. The petals should look as if they are all bowing towards the center.
- Attach the first two petals around the flower as shown in Figs. d and e.

- Next attach the 5 layers of petals as follows: For the first 3 layers, attach 5, 9, 13 of petal A (5 in the first layer, 9 in the 2nd layer, etc., working from the inside out).
- For the 2 outer layers, attach 17 and 21 of petal B. Link the petals of each layer in sequence (Fig. e) with thin florist wire (see instructions for a many-petaled flower if needed, pages 28 to 29).
- As you arrange the layers one by one around the center, rotate them slightly from the previous layer, so that the petals no longer fall exactly on top of each other.

Leaf

Color: Dark green. Method: Formula 2, frilled edge, on a stick ⅜" (1 cm) wide. Length of loops on stick: 2¾" (7 cm). Length of leaf: 1¾" (4.5 cm).

Assembly

- Make some groups of 3 leaves on side stems. Attach the bud at the top of a stem and attach some leaf groups below it (Fig. g), wrapping down the stems with dark green wool.
- Attach a flower to the top of a stem and attach side stems with leaf groups below the flower. (Fig. h).

Decorative chrysanthemum. **a.** Wrapping the wire for center of flower. **b.** The bent center. **c.** A petal, pinched double and bent backwards. **d.** Attaching one petal to a flower center. **e.** Inner layer of petals on a flower. **f.** A few linked petals being added to a flower. **g.** A closed bud and some leaves attached. **h.** A finished flower with leaves in groups of three.

Blood-Twig Dogwood

(*Cornus sanguinea*)

The blood-twig dogwood is a good accompaniment to other flowers in an arrangement. The blood-twig dogwood (also called the common European dogwood, the red dogwood, and pedwood) is a member of the dogwood family. Dogwoods are easily grown and require little maintenance, so they are garden favorites. The blood-twig dogwood has bright red-brown branches, white flowers, and dark blue-black berries. When the leaves fall off, the bright red-brown branches add color to the garden.

Wool: Reddish brown
Tools and supplies: Florist wire, PVAc glue

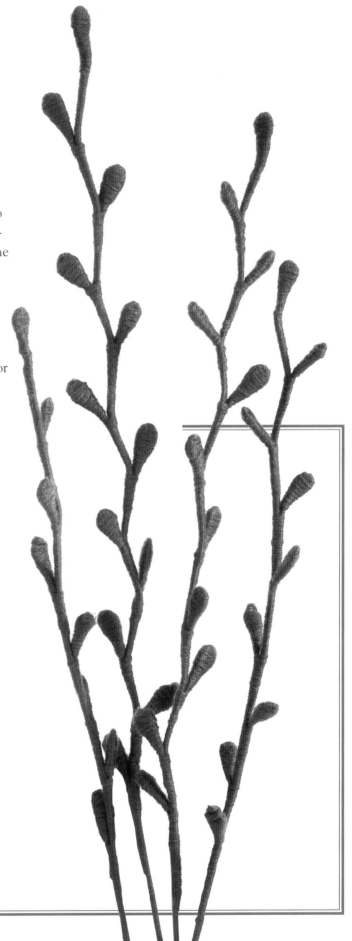

Preparation and Assembly

- Wind a length of wire about 4¾" (12 cm) long with brown wool (Fig. a) and bend it double. Continue covering this with a double strand of brown wool in an Egyptian-mummy fashion to make a "spoon" (Figs. b and c); then finish off with a dab of PVAc glue at the end of the wool.
- Prepare a sufficient number of these spoon shapes.
- Attach them in an alternating pattern to a florist wire stem (Fig. d), wrapping down the stem with reddish brown wool.
- Bend the stalk zigzag fashion to get a natural-looking twig (Fig. e).
- Make several twigs to use in arrangements with other flowers.

Blood-twig dogwood. **a.** Winding brown wool for start of twig spoon. **b.** The twig spoon, starting to wrap. **c.** The twig spoon, wrapped. **d.** The spoons attached in an alternating pattern. **e.** The bent twig.

Foxtail Lily

(*Eremurus*)

The foxtail lily, or desert candle, blooms with a profusion of tiny yellow flowers in large racemes on its central spike.

Tools: Pencil, sewing needle
Wool: Green 2-ply wool; yellow undivided worsted-weight wool for buds and flowers
Other: Yellow ready-made stamens (you may need a few hundred), yellow sewing thread, florist wire, heavy all-purpose wire for main stem, florist tape, PVAc glue

Bud

- Make the bud of 2 loops of yellow undivided wool, wrapped on a pencil.
- Tie the yellow loops together with yellow sewing thread (see Figs. a and b). Trim off close to tie.
- Wrap around the bottom of each bud with green wool to form a calyx. For smaller buds, cover more of the yellow loops; leave more yellow showing for larger buds.

Flower

The individual flower resembles that of the forget-me-not, but unlike the latter, it has 6 long stamens. To make the flowers, we use the thick yarn method, because as working material we use unseparated rayon yarn that is about the weight of knitting worsted.

- Bind 6 stamens on a 2" (5 cm) long wire.
- Thread a needle with yellow sewing thread. Take yellow undivided yarn, wind it once around a pencil, and tie it closed with yellow sewing thread to be the first petal. Leave it on the pencil.
- Wind the yarn around the pencil again; bind it with thread for the second petal, and so on, until there are 4 petals linked with thread on the pencil.
- Slide the petals off the pencil.
- Attach 2 or 3 stamens to a florist wire. Wrap the 5 petals around the stamen, and bind them in place with thread (Fig. c).

- Wrap around the stem below the flower with green wool to make a calyx, and keep wrapping down the stem for another inch (2.5 cm); later this stem will be joined to the main stem with many other flowers and buds.

Assembly

- Prepare a heap of buds and flowers.
- Arrange them in a densely placed fashion all around the main stem of heavy all-purpose wire.
- Bind the buds near the top of the stem and bind flowers together in groups of two and three; see photo and Fig. d.

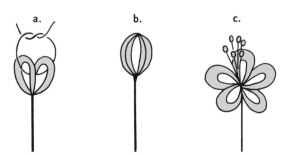

Foxtail lily. **a.** Tieing the loops for the bud. **b.** The finished bud. **c.** A flower, showing the stamens with petals around them. **d.** The finished foxtail lily.

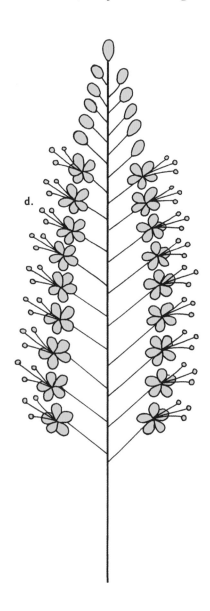

Heath

(Erica)

Heath bears erect budlike flowers; there is a stamen like a cat's whisker protruding out of each.

Tools: Yarn needle, sewing needle, cardboard strip ¾" (2 cm) wide
Wool: Violet, black, and green
Other supplies: Black sewing thread for stamens; violet thread for buds, PVAc glue or other strong craft glue, florist wire, thick all-purpose wire for main stem, florist tape

Budlike Flower

- Make a knot in the center of three 3" (7.5 cm) lengths of 2-ply black wool.
- Thread a needle with black sewing thread. With the sewing needle, stab through the knot; cut off the excess thread, leaving about a ½" (1 cm) tail of black thread behind (see Fig. a). Set aside.
- Wind the violet wool around a 3" (7.5 cm) wide cardboard. Cut through all the wool at the edges of the cardboard so you have 3" strands of wool.
- Continue by making a closed bud with violet wool around the black center. To do this, first, dab the tip of a short florist wire with PVAc glue, and stab it through the black wool knot. Then add more glue to the wire and distribute the lavender wool strands evenly around the wire, as shown in Fig. b, so most of the length is above the wire end, with the black knot inside. Tie the strands around the wire with violet wool, all the way up to the tip of the wire.

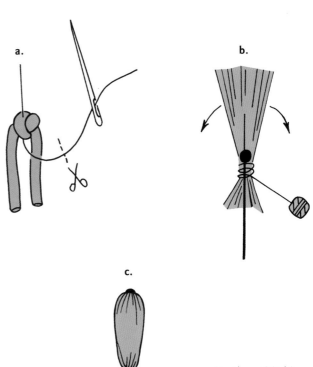

Heath. **a.** Stitching through a knot of black wool to start a flower. **b.** Securing wool strands around center knot. **c.** Trimming off ends of wool strands.

- Pull the wool strands downwards around the wire and secure them around the wire with violet thread (Fig. c). The black knot will show at the top of the flower. Trim off the wool strand ends that extend down the stem below the wrapping.
- Wrap the binding and stem with green florist tape to give the flower an all-in-one appearance (Fig. d).
- Wind a calyx of green wool around the base of the flower (Fig. e). Later this will attach to the main stem.
- Prepare many flowers the same way.

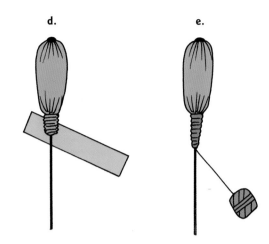

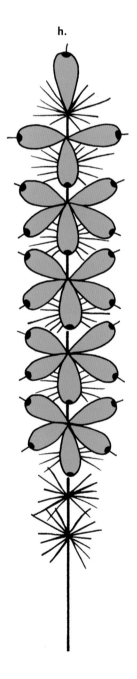

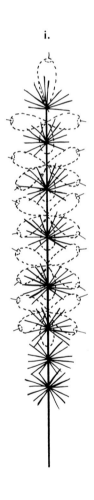

Heath. **d.** Wrapping bottom of flower with florist tape. **e.** Making a calyx below the flower. **f.** Winding wool for leaves. **g.** Tieing the wound leaf wool together. **h.** Main stem with flowers arranged on front. **i.** Back view, showing leaves.

Leaves

- Wind green wool around the cardboard (Fig. f).
- Thread a yarn needle with green and tie the loops together with wool at one end to make a leaf bunch (Figs. f and g) by running the yarn under the loops. Tie yarn ends together and slide the leaf bunch off the cardboard.
- Make a lot of leaves the same way.

Assembly

- Tie the first flower on the top of the main stem of all-purpose wire. Fasten 2 bunches of leaves directly below it, but don't cut the leaves through. Not yet!
- Bind 4 to 6 flower stems together, after wrapping them with green wool, and place them below the leaves. Wrap down the stem with green wool as you go. Arrange the flower groups as in Fig. h, tightly packed on the front of the stem; attach the leaves only at the back (Fig. i). In this manner add flowers and leaves to the entire stem.
- Then cut the outer ends of the leaf loops through with scissors to make fringe-like leaves.

Gum Tree

(*Eucalyptus leucoxylon*)

The gum tree is native to Australia. Its large, bright-colored flowers are very attractive to nectar-feeding birds.

Tools: Knitting needle size US 10 (UK 4, or 6 mm), ⅜" (1 cm) wide stick for making calyx
Wool: Light green, dark green, purple, scarlet
Other supplies: Florist wire, all-purpose galvanized wire, florist tape, green sewing thread to match wools, PVAc glue, cardboard strip 1½" (4 cm) wide

Flower

Colors: Scarlet and purple.
- Wind scarlet wool on a cardboard and cut loops on one side to make strands of wool. Do the same with purple wool.
- For each flower, twist a long florist wire around a bundle of strands with scarlet wool on the outside and purple wool on the inside to form a broom shape (Fig. a).
- Wrap the base of the flower with green thread to secure it (Fig. b). The purple wool will then appear at the center of the flower.
- Attach a light-green closed calyx to conceal the bindings of the broom-shaped flower, and trim the ends of the flower with scissors to even out (Fig. c).
- Wrap down the stems with green wool partway and join some in groups of two flowers (see photo).

Calyx

Color: Light green. Method: See closed calyx, Fig. 1-16.

Leaves

UNOPENED LEAF

- For each unopened leaf, wind light green wool around 4" (10 cm) of florist wire. Bend it double and wind with

Gum tree. **a.** Starting to make the flower with twisted wire. **b.** Wrapping the binding of the strands with thread. **c.** After the calyx is attached, evening off the flower.

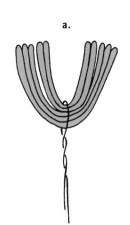

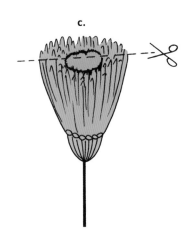

wool again, as for making the blood-twig dogwood (see page 73). Make 2 more leaf wires the same way.

- Bind 3 leaf wires together for the top of the main stalk. (The top will be hanging down in the final position.)

LARGE LEAF

Color: Dark green. Method: Knitting needle method, Formula 4, smooth edge, with needle size US 10 (UK 4, or 6 mm). Length of loops on needle: 8" (20 cm). Length of leaf: 4" (10 cm). Make each leaf on a separate stem. Then wrap down each leaf stem with light green wool partway.

Assembly

- Putting the unopened leaves at the start of the grouping (see photo), attach some large leaves together in a

leaf stem, which will hang down.
- Wrap down each flower stem partway with light green wool and join flower stems together in groups of 2 or 3. Attach some leaves to the flower stems.
- Then join the flower stem to the main stem. See photo for guidance.

Santo Sour Cherry
(*Eucryphia glutinosa*)

Here is another example of a flower with an even number of petals. The santo sour cherry has a profusion of stamens and bold white petals. It is native to Chile.

Tools: Sticks ⅝" (1.5 cm) and 1" (2.5 cm) wide
Wool: White, green
Other supplies: Yellow ready-made stamens with brown tips, florist wire, all-purpose galvanized wire for main stem, florist tape, sewing thread, PVAc glue

Santo sour cherry, one flower and a leaf.

Flower Petal

Color: White. Number: 4 petals per flower. Method: Formula 3, smooth edge, on a stick 1" (2.5 cm) wide. Length of loops on stick: 3½" (8.75 cm). Length of petal: 2" (5 cm).

FLOWER ASSEMBLY
- Tie a bunch of stamens together with florist wire. Arrange the petals around them, binding them in place, as shown in photo.
- Bind down the stem with dark green wool for about 3" (7.5 cm) on each flower.

Leaf

Color: Green. Method: Formula A, frilled edge, on a stick ⅝" (1.5 cm) wide. Length of loops on stick: 3¾" (9.5 cm). Length of leaflet: 2¾" (7 cm).

- The leaves are compound. Make about 35 leaflets. Wrap each leaflet for about ½" (1 cm) on its stem with dark green wool.
- To assemble, start with one leaflet at the top of a florist wire leaf stem, and then arrange two pairs of leaflets opposite each other on the same leaf stem.
- Make about 7 compound leaf stems this way.

Assembly

- Attach a flower to the top of a main stem that is all-purpose wire.
- Wrap down the main stem with dark green wool, adding leaf stems and flowers to the main stem as you go. See photo and figure for guidance.

Cushion Spurge
(Euphorbia polychrome)

The cushion spurge has buds and 3 layers of petal-like bracts (A, B, C) on each flower; from the inner to the outer they increase in size. For a harmonious effect, it is best to begin with lemon yellow for the flower buds and to use greenish yellow and ever greener hues of the same value for the bracts, using dark green for the leaves.

Tools: Sticks ³⁄₁₆", ⅜", and ¾" (0.5, 1, and 2 cm) wide
Wool: Lemon yellow, light greenish yellow, medium greenish yellow, dark greenish yellow, dark green
Other supplies: Lemon yellow ready-made stamens, florist tape, florist wire, thick all-purpose galvanized wire for main stem, sewing thread to match wool, PVAc glue

Closed Flower Buds

Color: Lemon yellow. Method: See closed bud (Fig. 1-11), and make 8 to 11 buds for each flower.

Bracts

BRACT A

Color: Light greenish yellow. Number: 3 bracts per flower. Method: Formula 2, smooth edge, on a stick ³⁄₁₆" (0.5 cm) wide. Length of loops on stick: 2" (5 cm). Length of bract: 1¼" (3 cm).

b.

a.

Cushion spurge. **a.** A bud with stamens positioned around it. **b.** The cushion spurge with bracts and leaves attached. Note: Only half the bracts are shown in diagram; they actually go all around the buds (see photo).

BRACT B
Color: Medium greenish yellow. Number:
5 bracts per flower. Method: Formula 2
smooth edge, on a stick ⅜" (1 cm) wide.
Length of loops on stick: 2¾" (7 cm).
Length of bract: 1¾" (4.5 cm).

BRACT C
Color: Dark greenish yellow. Number: 7
bracts per flower. Method: Formula 1,
smooth edge, on a stick ⅜" (1 cm) wide.
Length of loops on stick: 3⅛" (8 cm).
Length of bract: 2³⁄₁₆" (5.5 cm).

Flower Assembly

- Tie a bunch of stamens on the main stem at about 2" (5 cm) down from the base of the first attached bud (Fig. a). Then tie the buds together in a group on the stem, with 8 to 11 flower buds in a group.
- Next attach 3 bracts of the lightest greenish yellow (Bract A) around the main stem, then follow with the 5 bracts of the medium greenish yellow (Bract B).
- Rotate the bracts with each layer so they don't all fall just underneath each other.
- Attach 7 bracts of the darkest greenish yellow (Bract C) last; see Fig. b.

Leaves

Color: Dark green. Method: Formula 1, smooth edge, on a stick ¾" (2 cm) wide. Length of loops on stick: 4" (10 cm). Length of leaf: 3⅛" (8 cm).

Assembly

- Attach each flower bud to the main, all-purpose galvanized wire stem, and position so flower buds form a rounded shape on the top of the stem.
- Attach leaves directly to stem, opposite each other, or in groups of two or three (see photo).

Poinsettia
(*Euphorbia pulcherrima*)

The poinsettia is a strange flower. The center of the poinsettia is made of a bunch of what look like buds and half-open buds with calyxes, which in fact are the real flowers. The red petal-like structures we see are not flower petals at all, but red bracts.

Tools: Sticks ⅜", ½", ⅝", and ¾" (1, 1.3, 1.5, and 2 cm) wide
Wool: Bright red, yellow, medium green, dark green
Other supplies: Florist wire, all-purpose galvanized wire, florist tape, green sewing thread, PVAc glue

"Buds" (Flowers)

HALF-OPEN BUD

- A half-open bud has red and yellow wool in the center clasped by a green closed calyx.
- To make a half-open bud, bind together a number of red and yellow wool strands, each about 1" (2.5 cm) long, with florist wire, in the method of making the flower for the gum tree (see page 80); however, the flowers here are smaller.
- Then attach a closed calyx around it as shown in Fig. a; see below for calyx.
- Trim the protruding red and yellow wool level with scissors, just above the braided edge of the calyx. The result is shown in Fig. b.

- Bind a number of these buds together.
- Wrap down the stem of the bud a short way with light green wool.
- For each poinsettia make 9 half-open buds.

CLOSED BUD

Color: Green. Method: Make a closed calyx with nothing inside it; see closed calyx, Fig. 1-16. Sew the braided side of the calyx closed to make a bud. Wrap down the stem a short way with light green wool. For each poinsettia, make 3 closed buds.

Calyx

Color: Green. Method: See closed calyx (Fig. 1-16), and use a stick ½" (1.3 cm) wide. Number of loops on stick: 17.

Bracts

BRACT A

Color: Red. Number: 6 or 7 per flower. Method: Formula 2, smooth edge, on a stick ⅜" (1 cm) wide. Length of loops on stick: 2¾" (7 cm). Length of bract: 1¾" (4.5 cm).

BRACT B

Color: Red. Number: 9 to 11 per flower. Method: Formula 1, smooth edge, on a stick ⅝" (1.5 cm) wide. Length of loops on stick: 3⅜" (8.5 cm). Length of bracts: 2½" (6.5 cm).

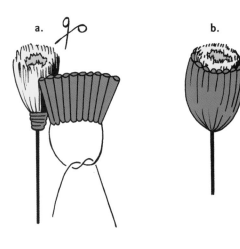
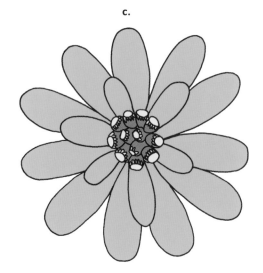

Poinsettia. **a.** An open bud, with a closed calyx in front of it, not yet attached. **b.** The finished open bud. **c.** Top view of a poinsettia with bracts attached. **d.** A leaf.

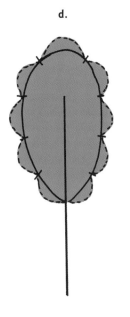

Leaf

Color: Dark green. Method: Formula 1, smooth edge, on a stick ¾" (2 cm) wide. Length of loops on stick: 4" (10 cm). Length of leaf: 3⅛" (8 cm). Make 2 leaves for each poinsettia.

Assembly

- Bind all the buds together on a thick stem with light green wool.
- Attach 6 to 7 of bract A around the buds; then attach 9 to 11 of bract B around them. The finished poinsettia can be seen from overhead in Fig c.
- Bind the leaves beneath the group of buds and bracts with dark green wool.
- Stretch the braided side of each leaf with your fingers at even intervals. The edge of the leaf will become slightly scalloped (Fig. d).

Fern

(Pteridophyta)

Although the fern is not a flowering plant, it is quite useful in flower arranging. As many ferns are epiphytes, we see them very frequently in the company of other epiphytes such as orchids. Ferns are very easy to make and consist of a bunch of frilled stalks.

Tools: Knitting needle size US 10 (UK 4, or 6 mm)
Wool: Green
Other supplies: Florist glue, florist tape, green thread, PVAc glue

Making the Fern

- We can make frills for the fern fronds by the knitting needle method (smooth edge, without a wire on the needle) using two strands of 2-ply wool. The fern can be made any length. To determine the length of the assisting wool, it is best to make a test piece first, to be sure it is long enough. The length also depends on how dense we want the frills on the stalk to be. (See how-to section of book for explanation of assisting wool if needed.)

- Put as many loops on the knitting needle as needed for the length you want.

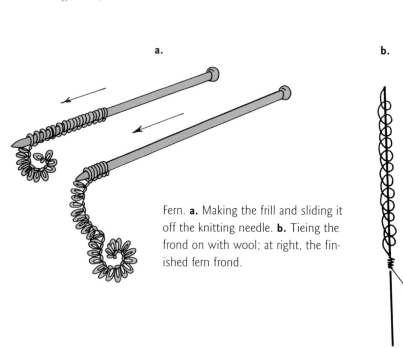

Fern. **a.** Making the frill and sliding it off the knitting needle. **b.** Tieing the frond on with wool; at right, the finished fern frond.

- A piece of florist wire will become a stalk. Glue one end of the frill of loops to what will become the top of the stalk; slide the loops down off the needle very slowly and carefully, little by little, while spiraling them around the stalk (Fig. a). Don't cut the frill off the ball of wool yet.
- Take care not to pull the looped wool. Wind it loosely around the wire until all the frill is used up.
- If the frill does not cover the desired length of wire, don't panic! Make another frill and glue that next to where you left off.
- Dab the end of the wool with PVAc glue to secure it and prevent it from unwinding.
- Wind the rest of the stem below the frill with green wool as usual (Fig. b) to finish one frond of the fern.
- Fronds can be assembled in bunches with green thread and florist tape. They go well with other flowers.

Crested Gentian

(*Gentiana septemfida*)

This hardy perennial has blue flowers in early summer. It is originally from the Caucasus.

Tools: Stick ⅜" (1 cm) wide, knitting needle US size 10 (UK 4, or 6 mm)
Wool: Prussian blue, moss green
Other supplies: White ready-made stamens, florist wire, all-purpose galvanized wire, florist tape, sewing thread to match wool, PVAc glue

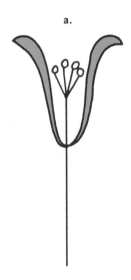

a.

b.

Crested gentian. **a.** Cross-section of flower, showing stamens. **b.** The finished crested gentian.

Flower Petal

Color: Prussian blue. **Number:** 5 per flower. **Method:** Formula 1, smooth edge, on a stick ⅜" (1 cm) wide. Length of loops on stick: 6" (15 cm). Length of petal: 3½" (9 cm).

Calyx

Color: Moss green. **Method:** Leafed calyx (see Fig. 1-19), knitting needle method, Formula 4, smooth edge, on a knitting needle size US 10 (UK 4, or 6 mm). Length of loops on needle: 4" (10 cm). Length of leaf of calyx: 2" (5 cm).

Leaf

Color: Moss green. **Method:** Formula 1, smooth edge, on a stick ⅜" (1 cm) wide. Length of loops on stick: 6" (15 cm). Length of leaf: 3½" (9 cm). Make 9 to 11 leaves for each main stem.

Assembly

- Bind 8 stamens in the center on all-purpose galvanized wire and attach 5 petals lower down on the main stem around them to make a flower (Fig. a); curl the upper section of the long flower petals outwards in such a way as to form a bell shape.
- Bind the calyx of 5 sepals at the base of each flower (Fig. b).
- Group 4 flowers in a cluster at the top of the stem, tieing them together 2" (5 cm) down their stems.
- Arrange and attach some leaves in a whorled formation around the stem just below where the flowers join.
- Wrap the stem downward with green wool, adding leaves opposite each other as you go.

Closeup of flower, showing calyx.

Sunflower

(Helianthus)

The sunflower is a composite flower. Its flower head is really made up of many small florets, although people usually call them petals.

Tools: Sticks ⅜" (1 cm) and 1" (2.5 cm) wide, crochet hook
Wool: Yellow, green, brown
Other supplies: 2 circles of cardboard of diameter 3½" (9 cm) and 1 circle of cardboard of diameter 2½" (6 cm), florist wire, florist tape, sewing thread to match wool, PVAc glue, sturdy all-purpose galvanized wire padded with tissue paper for stem

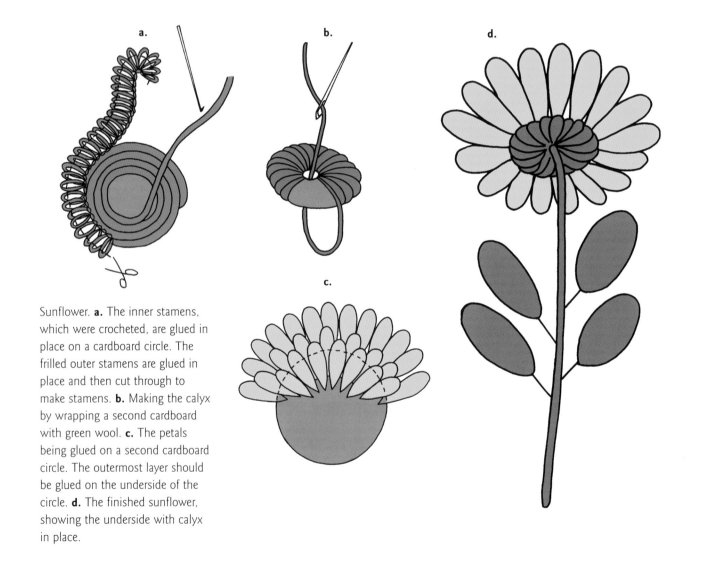

Sunflower. **a.** The inner stamens, which were crocheted, are glued in place on a cardboard circle. The frilled outer stamens are glued in place and then cut through to make stamens. **b.** Making the calyx by wrapping a second cardboard with green wool. **c.** The petals being glued on a second cardboard circle. The outermost layer should be glued on the underside of the circle. **d.** The finished sunflower, showing the underside with calyx in place.

Flower Petal

Color: Yellow. Number: 70 per flower.
Method: Formula 1, smooth edge, on
a stick ⅜" (1 cm) wide. Length of
loops on stick: 4⅜" (11 cm).
Length of petal: 2¾" (7 cm).

Stamens

INNER STAMENS

Color: Brown. Method: Crochet
a long chain in brown with a triple
strand of wool. Glue it in a
tight spiral on the 3½" (9 cm)
cardboard (see Fig. a, center).

OUTER STAMENS

Color: Brown. Method: See the frilled
calyx, Method 2 (Fig. 1-18b).

• Cast on stitches of a length that will
  fit twice around the perimeter of the
  inner stamens' 3½" cardboard circle.

• Glue the double row of loops cast on
  along the border of the circle of inner
  stamens already attached to the cardboard. Then cut the loops through to
  make the stamens (Fig. a).

Calyx

Color: Green. Take the 2½" (6 cm) circle
of cardboard, make a hole in the center,
and wrap the whole cardboard with
green wool (see Fig. b).

ends extend a little less than the outer ends of the first layer of petals.

- Glue on the third (innermost) layer of 19 petals on the right side of the circle. Let dry overnight (Fig. c).
- Glue the cardboard circle with the stamens onto the front of the circle with the petals.
- Slide the thick main stem through the green-wrapped calyx circle, and glue the calyx and stem to the underside of the petal circle with PVAc glue (see photo and Fig. d for guidance). Let dry.
- Wind down the padded stem with green wool, continuing from the calyx, and attach the leaves in an alternate pattern as you go.

Leaf

Color: Green. Method: Formula 1, smooth edge, on a stick 1" (2.5 cm) wide. Length of loops on stick: 4⅞" (12.5 cm). Length of leaf: 4" (10 cm). Make about 4 leaves for each stem.

Assembly

- Each layer of the flower petals should be linked with wire (see Fig. 1-15 for reference).
- Glue the outer layer of 27 petals with PVAc glue to form the outer border of the second 3½" (9 cm) cardboard circle. The outer layer of petals should go on the underside of the circle.
- Turn the circle right-side up. Then glue on the second layer of petals (24 petals), to the right side, so their outer

Back of sunflower, showing calyx.

Sea Buckthorn
(*Hippophae rhamnoides*)

Native to China and Russia, the sea buckthorn is being cultivated in other countries as well, for its golden orange fruit, which are a source of vitamins and other nutrients.

Tools: Knitting needle, US size 9 (UK size 5, or 5.5 mm)

Wool: Dark yellow, dark brown, moss green

Other supplies: Brown tissue paper, all-purpose galvanized wire, florist wire, thread to match the wool

Berry

Color: Dark yellow: Method: Refer to instructions for making a berry and Fig. 1-11. The berries are about 1" (2.5 cm) tall on short stems wrapped with dark brown wool below the berry.

Branches and Stems

Color: Dark brown. Use tissue-paper-wrapped all-purpose galvanized wire for the main stem; the main stems are wrapped with dark brown wool as you add leaves and berries.

Leaf

Color: Moss green. Method: Knitting needle method, Formula 4, smooth edge, on a knitting needle US size 9 (UK size 5, or 5.5 mm). Length of loops on needle: 6" (15 cm). Length of leaf: 3" (7.5 cm).

Assembly

- Prepare many leaves and berries.
- Starting at the top of a wire for a side branch, attach some leaves on alternate sides of the branch, wrapping down the branch with brown wool as you work.
- Then attach some berries as shown in the diagram and photo. Continue wrapping down the branch with brown wool.
- Create several side branches the same way, and join them to the tissue-wrapped all-purpose galvanized wire for the main stem, attaching side branches with brown wool. See photo for guidance.

The finished sea buckthorn.

Hydrangea

(*Hydrangea macrophylla*)

The hydrangea has florets made in the same way as those of the lilac, but of blue wool. Because they are arranged in a different way from the lilac, they resemble a different flower.

Tools: Knitting needle size US 10 (UK 4, or 6 mm), stick ¾" (2 cm) wide
Wool: Light blue, green
Other supplies: Ready-made light blue stamens, florist tape, florist wire, sewing thread to match wool, PVAc glue, tissue-paper padded all-purpose thick galvanized wire or stick for main stem

Floret Petal

Color: Light blue. Number: 4 per floret.
Method: Knitting needle method,
Formula 4, smooth edge, on a knitting
needle size US 10 (UK 4, or 6 mm).
Length of loops on needle: 1½" (4 cm).
Length of petal: ¾" (2 cm). Prepare
many petals.

Florets and Floret Groups

- To make each floret, attach 3 stamens
  to a 4" (10 cm) florist wire stem.
- Position and tie 4 petals around the
  stamens.
- Wrap the stems from the petals
  together with light blue wool for 1½"
  (3.5 cm).
- Bind the florets together in groups of
  3 florets with light blue wool, wrapping down stems for another inch
  (2.5 cm) to make a floret group.

Leaf

Color: Green. Method: Formula 1,
smooth edge, on a stick ¾" (2 cm) wide.
Length of loops on stick: 4" (10 cm).
Length of leaf: 3⅛" (8 cm). Wrap leaf
stems with green wool for about 1"
(2.5 cm).

Assembly

The hydrangea consists of clusters of
4-petaled florets, packed tightly in a
round head called an umbel.

- On the thick main stem wire, arrange
  the floret groups in a tightly packed
  dome shape, binding them in place
  with light blue wool.
- Bind the leaves together in groups of
  3 with green wool, for about an inch
  (2.5 cm), keeping aside a few as single
  leaves.
- Attach the single leaves a few inches
  (5 or 7 cm) below the umbel of florets.
- Attach the leaf groups of 3 farther
  down on the padded main stem (see
  diagram and photo).

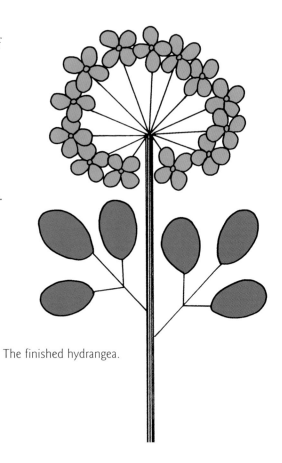

The finished hydrangea.

Crape Myrtle

(*Lagerstroemia indica*)

The crape myrtle has dainty florets massed in groups on the top of a stem that droops with their weight.

Tools: Knitting needle US size 9 (UK size 5, or 5.5 mm), stick ⅜" (1 cm) wide, sewing needle
Wool: Soft rose, yellowish green, olive green, dark green
Other supplies: Ready-made yellow stamens, florist wire, all-purpose galvanized wire, florist tape, sewing thread to match wools, PVAc glue

Floret

Color: Soft rose. **Method:** Knitting needle, frilled edge, on a knitting needle US size 9 (UK size 5, or 5.5 mm), strung with thin florist wire. Number of loops on needle: 24.

- To make a single floret, pull the ends of the wire that is on the length of the knitting needle together to form a circlet after the loops are cast on. The frilled edge forms the outer perimeter of the circlet. Twist the wire ends together to fasten the circlet and form the floret stem.
- Wrap the floret stem with yellowish green wool for about 1" (2.5 cm).
- Make many little florets this way.

Calyx

Color: Yellowish green. Method: Knitting needle method without a wire (smooth edge), knitting needle US size 9 (UK size 5, or 5.5 mm). Number of loops on needle: 36. Make one calyx for every 6 florets.

Leaf

Color: Dark green. Method: Formula 2, smooth edge, on a stick ⅜" (1 cm) wide. Length of loops on stick: 2¾" (7 cm). Length of leaf: 1¾" (4.5 cm).

Assembly

- Each floret is a little circlet of rose wool on a light green stem.
- Each floret grouping consists of 6 florets tied together, with a greenish yellow calyx at the base.
- To make a floret grouping, bind 6 stamens to a florist wire and arrange and attach 6 florets on their wool-wrapped stems around the stamens. Glue a calyx around the stamens (Fig. a).
- Bind the stems of the 6 florets together with olive green wool in a funnel shape below the calyx to make a floret group (see photo).
- Bind many floret groups on a main stem of heavy wire with olive green wool so they are on many sides of the stem.
- Keep adding more floret groupings as you work your way down the main stem.
- Add a few leaves on the main stem.
- Make a second spike of florets and bind it to the main stem.
- Make side stems with 5 leaves on them as shown in Fig. b, and bind them to the main stem.

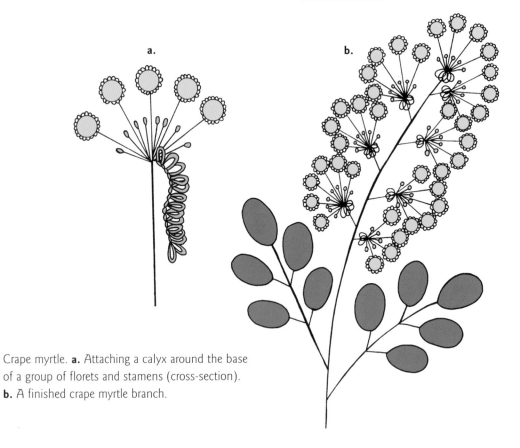

Crape myrtle. **a.** Attaching a calyx around the base of a group of florets and stamens (cross-section). **b.** A finished crape myrtle branch.

Forget-me-not

(Myosotis sylvatica)

The sticks we have used so far won't work well for the forget-me-not, with its tiny flower petals. Therefore we resort to another technique. We've called it the thick yarn method. We use undivided rayon yarn of about worsted weight to make the florets, as we did with the bouvardia.

Tools: Stick ¾" (2 cm) wide, pencil, sewing needle
Wool: Sky-blue undivided yarn, 2-ply moss green wool
Other: Yellow ready-made stamens, matching blue sewing thread, florist wire, florist tape, PVAc glue

Floret

Color: Sky-blue. **Number:** 5 petals per floret. **Method:** Thick yarn method of making the florets. Each floret has a single yellow stamen.

- Tie a single yellow stamen on a 2" (5 cm) long wire.
- Thread a needle with blue thread. Take blue undivided yarn, wind it once around a pencil, and tie it with blue sewing thread to be the first petal. Leave it on the pencil.
- Wind yarn around the pencil again; bind it with blue sewing thread for the second petal, and so on, until there are 5 petals linked with thread on the pencil.
- Slide the petals off the pencil.
- Wrap the 5 petals around the stamen and bind them in place with thread. Wind with thin blue wool a short way down the wire and cut the wool.

Bud

Color: Sky blue. **Method:** Make tiny closed buds by knotting sky blue wool.

Leaf

Color: Green. **Method:** Formula 1, smooth edge, on a stick ¾" (2 cm) wide. Length of loops on stick: 5½" (14 cm). Length of leaf: 4" (10 cm).

Assembly

- Attach buds and florets on a side stem, wrapping with green wool.
- Attach several side stems to the main stem.
- Add the leaves on alternating sides as shown in the diagram.

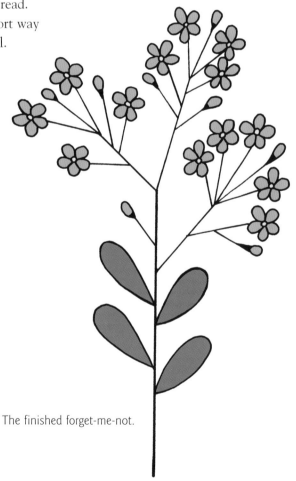

The finished forget-me-not.

Water Lily or Lotus

(*Nymphaea 'Escarboucle'*)

Water lilies have been cultivated for thousands of years for their beauty, as well as for food and for medicines. There are about 50 species of water lily.

Tools: Sticks ⅜" (1 cm) and ⅝" (1.5 cm) wide, sewing needle, yarn needle
Wool: Gold, carmine, dark green
Other: Yellow ready-made stamens, clear cellophane tape, yarn needle, dark green thread

Flower Petals

PETAL A
Color: Carmine. Number: 7 and 8 petals.
Method: Formula 1, smooth edge, on a stick ⅜" (1 cm) wide. Length of loops on stick: 4" (10 cm). Length of petal: 2½" (6.5 cm). These are for the 2 inner layers of petals.

PETAL B
Color: Carmine. Number: 7 and 9 petals.
Method: Formula 1, smooth edge, on a stick ⅝" (1.5 cm) wide. Length of loops on stick: 4⅞" (12.5 cm). Length of petal: 3⅜" (8.5 cm). These are for the 2 outer layers of petals.

Center of Flower

- Make a gold berry on a 4" (10 cm) stem (see How to make a berry, page 35)
- Press the yellow stamens onto clear sticky tape, close to each other (Fig. a). Cut away the bottom balls on the stamens with scissors (see Fig. a).
- Wrap the clear tape with stamens around the berry until all is wrapped around (Fig. b). You can see a top view of the berry with stamens around it in Fig. c.
- Bind the berry with red wool ½" (1 cm) down the stem.

Flower Assembly

- String each layer of petals between two wires (see Fig. 1-15), beginning with the innermost layer of seven A petals, (Fig. d) and bind them to the stem below the berry.
- Next attach the second layer of eight A petals. Rotate the layers so the petals don't fall right on top of each other.
- Follow with the third layer of eight B petals and finish with the outer layer of nine B petals.
- Curve the petals so they curl upwards. Bind the petal layers and stem with red wool and then with green wool and cut off the excess stem so it is only about 1" (2.5 cm) long.

Leaf Sections and Assembly

Color: Dark green. Number: 33 leaf sections. Method: Formula 1, smooth edge, on a stick ⅜" (1 cm) wide. Length of

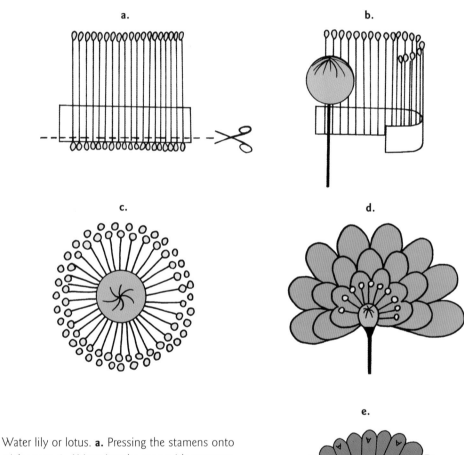

Water lily or lotus. **a.** Pressing the stamens onto sticky tape. **b.** Wrapping the tape with stamens around a berry. **c.** Top view of berry with stamens around it. **d.** View of half of a water lily, with 3 layers of petals in place. **e.** Leaf sections tacked together so alternate sections (A sections) overlap others.

loops on stick: 7¼" (18 cm). Length of a section: 4⅛" (10.5 cm).

- Make a leaf section on the stick as you would a leaf or petal. Bend in half so section is long and narrow.
- Twist the wire ends of each section around themselves and cut off excess wire.
- To make the leaf from the sections, thread a yarn needle with dark green wool. String the leaf sections together with wool, passing through the rounded side of each leaf section in a running stitch. Join all the leaf sections together this way, but don't stitch the last leaf section to the first section. Leave them detached so you will have a split circle for the leaf.

- Working with the wire-ends side of each leaf section, tack every other section (alternate sections) together with thread in a layer to become the center of the leaf. Then tack together the remaining leaf sections on their wire ends in a lower layer. Now some sections on their outer ends will appear to be overlapping the others (Fig. e).

Assembly

- Sew the flower to the leaf with green wool.
- Protect the bottom of the leaf by gluing on green paper or felt, cut in the shape of the leaf.

Pernettya
(*Pernettya mucronata*)

The pernettya, native to South America, New Zealand, and Tasmania, bears many showy berries that may range from deep burgundy to red, rose, pink, or even white. But don't eat its berries—they're poisonous. Pernettya grows as a shrub and forms a dense thicket of wiry stems, growing as tall as 3 feet (90 cm). It has glossy dark green leaves and small white flowers. Some people use pernettya as a hedge shrub, particularly as deer don't like it, so it can protect other plants. It can grow in full sun or partial shade. The berries are very decorative. It can also be grown in containers.

Tools: Stick ⅜" (1 cm) wide
Wool: Purple, medium green, dark brown
Other: Florist wire, florist tape, thick all-purpose galvanized wire for stem, PVAc glue, thread to match wool

Pernettya. The finished berry branch.

Berries

Color: Purple. **Method:** See How to make berries, page 35. Berries are like closed buds; see Fig. 1-11. Make the berries on 2" long (5 cm) florist wire stems, and wrap stems with medium green wool.

Leaf

Color: Medium green. **Method:** Formula 2, smooth edge, on a stick ⅜" (1 cm) wide. Length of loops on stick: 2⅜" (6 cm). Length of leaf: 1½" (4 cm).

Assembly

Arrange and attach the berries and leaves as in diagram and photograph. Start with opposite pairs of leaves, attached directly to the branches. Use medium weight wire for the side stems and thicker all-purpose galvanized wire for the main stem. Wrap stems with dark brown wool.

Redflowering Currant

(Ribes sanguineum)

The redflowering currant has racemes of drooping tubular flowers and buds. It is native to the western United States.

Tools: Stick ⅜" (1 cm), knitting needle size US 10 (UK 4, or 6 mm), piece of cardboard 2⅜" (6 cm) wide
Wool: Red, green
Other supplies: Ready-made white stamens, florist wire, heavy all-purpose galvanized wire for stem, florist tape, glue, sewing thread to match wool

Bud

Color: Red. Method: See How to make a closed bud (Fig. 1-11). Make several buds, each on its own thin wire stem about 5" (12.5 cm) long. Wrap the lower part of the bud and an inch (2.5 cm) of the stem with green wool (see photo).

Flower Petals

Color: Red. Number: 5 per flower. Method: Knitting needle method, Formula 4, smooth edge, on a knitting needle size US 10 (UK 4, or 6 mm). Length of loops on needle: 2½" (6 cm). Length of petal: 1¼" (3 cm).

Making a Flower

- Attach 6 stamens to a thin wire stem and bind 5 petals around them. Leave petals upright for now. Set it aside.
- To make the throat of the flower, wind about 8 turns of red wool around the

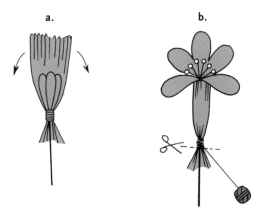

Redflowering currant. **a.** After the wool strands for the flower throat are attached over the petals all around, bend them down. **b.** Trim off any excess wool after the strands for the throat are bound to the stem. **c.** A branch of flowers.

cardboard, and cut the wool through along both edges of the cardboard.

- Distribute the red strands around the flower petals, binding them around the stem and petals so that most of their length extends up and about ½" (1.3 cm) extends below the binding (see Fig. a).
- Then pull the strands of wool down all around the stamens and petals on the stem. Bind the strands to the stem of the flower with green wool to make the throat of the blossom. Cut off the excess wool below the binding (Fig. b). Wrap down the flower stem partway with green wool.
- Make many flowers the same way as above, each on its own individual stem.

Leaf

Color: Green. Method: Formula 1, smooth edge, on a stick ⅜" (1 cm) wide. Length of loops on stick: 3⅛" (8 cm). Length of leaf: 2³⁄₁₆" (5.5 cm).

- Make 15 leaves.
- Bind 3 leaves together and wrap a short way down around all 3 stems

together with green wool to make a leaf group.

- Make other leaf groups the same way.

Assembling the Flowering Branch

- Start assembling the branch with the flowers and buds at the top of a wire stem to become a side branch (Fig. c and photo). Add more flowers around the stem (see photo).
- Join one flower side branch to the top of a thick all-purpose galvanized wire stem for the main stem. Wrap down the stem with green wool, attaching groups of leaves and flowers, as in photo.

Rose

(Rosa)

Roses are among the most popular garden shrubs. There are thousands of kinds of roses. Roses are ancient symbols of love and beauty.

Tools: Sticks 1" and ⅝" (2.5 cm and 1.5 cm) wide
Wool: Red, green
Other supplies: Florist wire, florist tape, PVAc glue, thread to match wool

Flower Petal

Color: Red. Number: 10 per flower. Method: Formula 3, smooth edge, on a stick 1" (2.5 cm) wide. Length of loops on stick: 3⅜" (8.5 cm). Length of petal: 2" (5 cm).

Calyx for Flower and Bud

Color: Green. Method: See frilled calyx, Method B (Fig. 1-18). Make a calyx for each flower and bud.

Flower Assembly

- Roll 2 petals together to form a flower center and attach them to a medium-weight all-purpose wire for a stem.
- Attach the next layer of petals one by one around the rolled center of the flower.
- In the same way, attach 4 or 5 outer petals around the ones you just attached. The petals should slightly overlap each other (Fig. a).

a.

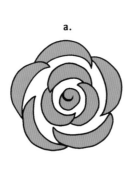

Rose. **a.** Overhead view of a rose flower. **b.** A finished rose.

b.

- Glue on the frilled calyx (made by method B) at the base of the flower (see Fig. 1-18).
- Shape the petals so the inner layers curve up around each other closely and the outer layers are more horizontal.

Bud

Color: Red. Method: A bud is made by rolling 1 or 2 red flower petals around themselves and binding them on a stem. Glue a frilled calyx below each bud.

Leaf

Color: Green. Method: Formula 2, smooth edge, on a stick ⅝" (1.5 cm) wide. Length of loops on stick: 2¾" (7 cm). Length of leaf: 2" (5 cm).

Assembly

- Keep each bud on a separate stem, as shown in photo, or on a side stem as shown in Fig. b.
- Assemble the leaves in groups of 3 or 5 on alternate sides of side stems (see photo). Wrap stems with florist tape and green wool.
- Attach the leaf side stems to the main stem of the bud or flower (see Fig. b and photo) by taping and wrapping with green wool.

African Violet

(*Saintpaulia ionantha*)

When you visit a sick friend, take a pot of these African violets with you. They are just great for that occasion.

Tools: Knitting needle size US 10 (UK 4, 6 mm), sticks ⅜" and 1³⁄₁₆" (1 cm and 3 cm) wide
Wool: Violet, green, yellow
Other supplies: Florist tape, florist wire, small pot with green florist foam (optional)

Stamen

Make a knot of 4 short strands of 2-ply yellow wool.

Flower Petals

PETAL A (NARROW PETAL)

Color: Violet. Number: 2 per flower. Method: Knitting needle method, Formula 4, smooth edge, on a needle size US 10 (UK 4, 6 mm). Length of loops on needle: 1¾" (4.5 cm).

PETAL B (WIDE PETAL)

Color: Violet. Number: 3 per flower. Method: Smooth edge, Formula 2, using stick ⅜" (1 cm) wide. Length of loops on stick: 1¾" (4.5 cm). Length of petal B: 1¼" (3 cm).

Flower Assembly

Fasten the yellow knot of wool (stamen) onto a stem about 5" (2.5 cm) long, and put the 5 petals around it, with 2 of petal A and 3 of petal B. Wrap with florist tape and green wool.

The finished African violet; each leaf, flower, and bud stem appears to grow directly from the ground.

Bud

Wrap three of petal A around each other so they are only partially open. Their wires will form the stem. Bind with florist tape and green wool, starting partway up the petals to suggest a calyx.

Leaf

Color: Green. Method: Formula 3, for round leaf, smooth edge, using stick ¾" (2 cm) wide and one wire on stick. Length of loops on stick: 2¾" (7 cm).

- See round leaf method, page 20 to 21, and Fig. 1-8a, but just use one wire on the stick.

- To position the stem of the leaf in the center, bend the stem from the center 90 degrees down from the leaf surface.
- Wrap the stem with florist tape and green wool.

Assembly

- Don't join the flower or bud stems together. Each flower and bud comes from the "ground" individually.
- Position the round leaves so they appear to sprout from the ground, each on its own wire stem.

Alpine Soldanella

(*Soldanella alpina*)

These alpine natives like a cool climate and damp fields. They are members of the primrose family. They are also known as alpine snowbells.

Tools: Knitting needle size US 10 (UK 4, or 6 mm), stick 1½" (4 cm) wide
Wool: Purple, medium green
Other supplies: Florist wire, all-purpose galvanized wire, florist tape, small flower pot, green floral foam, sewing thread to match wool, PVAc glue

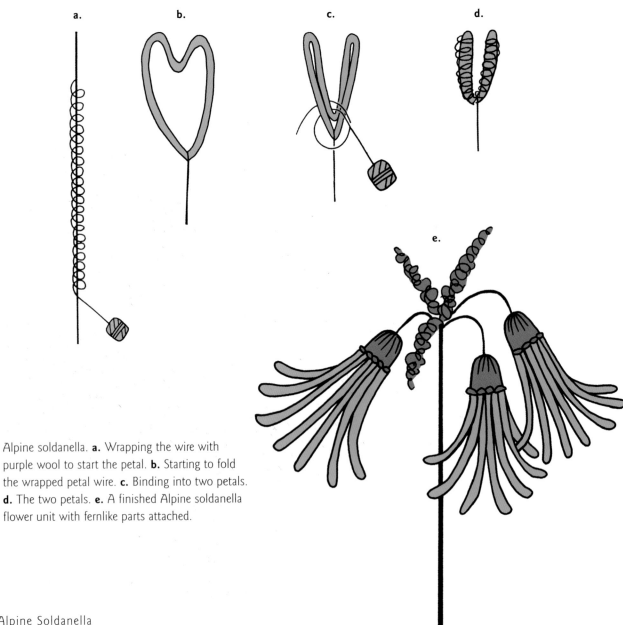

Alpine soldanella. **a.** Wrapping the wire with purple wool to start the petal. **b.** Starting to fold the wrapped petal wire. **c.** Binding into two petals. **d.** The two petals. **e.** A finished Alpine soldanella flower unit with fernlike parts attached.

Petals and Flower Assembly

- To make petals, wrap a 12" (30 cm) piece of florist wire with florist tape, and wind it with purple 2-ply wool, 2 times up and down the wire for about 3½" (9 cm) (Fig. a).
- Bend the wire as you would to make a leafed calyx (see Fig. b on this page; refer to leafed calyx instructions, page 34, if necessary) and wind each half again with purple wool (Fig. c) so that we have now made 2 petals (Fig. d).
- Make 2 petals the same way on each of 5 more wires for a total of 12 petals.
- Bind all 12 petals together at the unfinished wire end to make a flower.
- Make and attach a closed calyx of green wool (see closed calyx on page 30 to 31) at the base of each flower. Wrap down the stem of each flower for about 1½" (4 cm) with green wool.
- Make more flowers the same way.

Fernlike Parts

- Using green wool, make short fernlike parts, wrapping florist wire about 1" (2.5 cm) with a short fern frill (see instructions for Fern, page 90).
- Make 3 fern frills for each flower grouping.

Leaf

Color: Green. Method: Round leaf, Formula 3, smooth edge, on a stick 1¼" (3 cm) wide, using only 1 wire on the stick. Length of loops on stick: 4" (10 cm). Length of leaf: 2¼" (6.5 cm).

Assembly

- Bind 3 or 4 flowers together about 1½" (4 cm) down on their stems onto a thick all-purpose galvanized wire, including 3 short fernlike parts; strengthen the unit with all-purpose galvanized wire about 6" (15 cm) long to make a thicker stem. Wrap all together with florist tape and green wool (see Fig. e and photo).
- Make a lot of leaves, each on its own short stem, and stick each leaf stem individually into the foam so it appears to come out of the ground (see photo).

Salt Cedar

(*Tamarix pentandra*)

The flowers and the leaves of the salt cedar consist entirely of fernlike structures. The salt cedar gives off excess salt crystals from openings in its salty leaves.

Tools: Knitting needle US size 10 (UK size 4, or 6 mm)
Wool: Soft rose, moss (olive) green
Other supplies: Florist tape, florist wire, all-purpose galvanized wire, matching thread, PVAc glue

Frilly Flower Stalks

Color: Soft rose. Method: Like fern (see page 90).

- Make 3" (7.5 cm) long rose frills to wind around medium weight florist wire as described below, using the knitting needle method (smooth edge, without a wire) and working with two strands of 2-ply wool. To determine the length of the assisting wool, it is best to make a test piece first, to be sure it is long enough. (See Basics section of book for explanation of assisting wool if needed.)
- Put as many loops on the knitting needle as needed for the 3" (7.5 cm) length frill.
- A piece of florist wire will become a flower stalk. Glue one end of the frill to what will become the top of the stalk, and slide the loops down off the needle little by little, while spiraling them around the stalk. As you work, slide the loops slowly and very carefully off the needle. See the diagrams with Fern (page 90) for reference. Don't cut the frill wool off the ball yet.
- Take care not to pull the wool. Wind it loosely around the wire until all the frill is used up.
- If the frill does not cover the desired length of wire, don't panic! Make another frill and glue that one next to where you left off.
- Dab the end of the wool with PVAc glue to secure it and prevent it from unwinding.
- Wind the rest of the stem below the frill with green wool as usual for about ½" (1 cm); leave the rest of the wire unwound for now. This finishes one flower stem.

Green Frilly Leaves

Color: Moss green. Make 2 or 3 shorter green frills, the same way you made the flower frills. They will be bound in low down on the branch.

Assembly

- Make many frilly flower stalks and assemble as shown in the diagram, binding them together with green wool to make a branch.
- Make another branch as before, joining to the first branch, and wrap both stems together with green wool. Add a few frilly leaves near the join and farther down the stem.

The completed salt cedar.

Waratah

(*Telopea speciosissima*)

The waratah or fire bush is the official floral emblem of New South Wales. What looks like one flower with many petals is really the flower head of a composite flower, made of a mass of many small flowers, with bracts lower down.

Tools: Sticks ⁵⁄₁₆" (75 mm), ⅜" (1 cm), and ¾" (2 cm) wide
Wool: Coral red, dark green
Other supplies: Florist wire, green florist tape, all-purpose galvanized wire, tissue paper

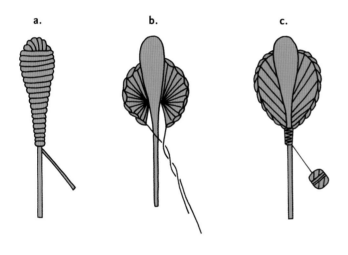

Waratah. **a.** Wrapping a spoon. **b.** Attaching a petal around a spoon with wire. **c.** Winding the yarn down the stem to secure the petal to the spoon. **d.** Cross-section of partially finished flower (not all bracts are attached).

Flower Head

The flower head includes 56 little flowers. Each little flower consists of a spoonlike shape (Fig. a) and a small petal clasping its base. Make them as described below.

SPOONS

Color: Coral red. Number: 56 + 5 per flower head. Method: See blood-twig dogwood, page 73, and Fig. a here.

SMALL PETALS

Color: Coral red. Number: 56 per flower head. Method: Formula 2, smooth edge, on a stick 5/16" (0.75 cm) wide. Length of loops on stick: 2½" (6.5 cm). Length of small petal: 1½" (4 cm).

LITTLE FLOWERS

- Make 56 little flowers, each consisting of 1 spoon and 1 small petal clasping its base (see Figs. b and c). Twist the petal wires around each spoon to fasten the petal around the spoon shape (Fig. b).
- Bend the spoons up like raised arms bent at the elbow.
- Below the petal, wrap the wire stem with red wool for about ½" (1 cm); see Fig. c.

BRACT

Color: Coral red. Number: 12 per flower head. Method: Formula 1, smooth edge, on a stick 3/8" (1 cm) wide. Length of loops on stick: 4¾" (12 cm). Length of bract: 3" (7.5 cm).

Leaf

Color: Dark green. Method: Formula 1, frilled edge, on a stick ¾" (2 cm) wide. Length of loops on stick: 5½" (14 cm). Length of leaf: 4" (10 cm).

Stem

Shape a stem on a round stick about 3/8" (1 cm) in diameter. Pad the upper section with tissue paper for about 6" (15 cm) so it is thick in the middle of the 6" and gets gradually thinner at the ends. Wrap with florist tape. Next, wind the thicker part of the stem with medium green wool.

Assembly

- Fasten 5 spoons without petals in a circle at the top of the padded stem.
- Then attach the following, using florist wire and medium green wool, working down the stem from the top.

See Fig. 1-15 for reference in preparing the small flowers between two wires:

- a layer of 6 small flowers
- a layer of 9 small flowers
- a layer of 15 small flowers
- a layer of 15 small flowers
- a layer of 11 small flowers

- At the base of the flower, arrange and attach 6 bracts in one layer and then another 6 bracts below them, using wire and medium green wool.
- After this is done, continue to wrap the stem with medium green wool, attaching the leaves as shown (see cross-section Fig. d and photo).

Geranium

(*Pelargonium*)

Geraniums have bright red little flowers (florets), arranged in an umbel; the florets radiate from the top of the stem like the spokes of an umbrella. At the base of the umbel, a cluster of closed and half-open buds hang. The leaves are round.

Tools: Knitting needle size US 10 (UK 4, or 6 mm), stick 1½" (4 cm) wide
Wool: Bright red, green, light green
Other supplies: Tissue paper, all-purpose galvanized wire, florist wire, florist tape, glue, pot for plant, green floral foam

Stamen

A knot made from a short length of 2-ply light-green wool will function as the stamen for each floret.

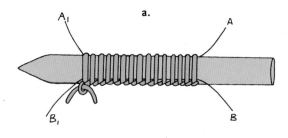

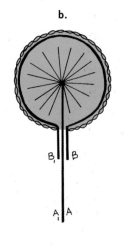

Geranium. **a.** To make the leaves, two heavy wires are used on the stick for support. **b.** Diagram of a round leaf, showing wire around edge (B₁ to B) and in center for stem (A₁ to A). **c.** Cross-section diagram of the finished plant.

Petal

Color: Bright red. Number: 5 petals per floret. Method: Knitting needle method, smooth edge, on a knitting needle US size 10 (UK 4, or 6 mm). Length of loops on needle: 1⁹⁄₁₆" (4 cm). Length of petal: ½" (2 cm).

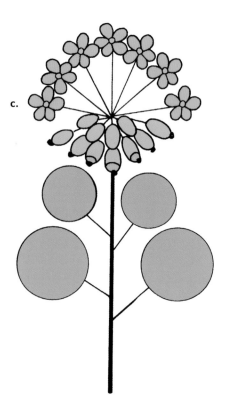

Floret Assembly

- To make a floret, attach the knotted stamen to a florist wire and then attach 5 petals around it.
- Wrap down the floret stem for about 1½" (4 cm) with green wool, forming a calyx and covering the wire partway. Make many florets the same way.

Buds

CLOSED BUD

Color: Dark green. Method: See closed buds, page 25. Make a number of closed buds, about ¾" (2 cm) long each. Wrap down the stem of each with dark green wool as for the floret.

Leaf

Color: Dark green. Method: Formula 3, round leaf method, smooth edge, on a stick 1½" (4 cm) wide. Length of loops on stick: 5½" (14 cm). Length of leaf: 3⅛" (8 cm).

- To make an extra large round leaf like this one, we need 2 rather thick florist wires instead of the usual one wire: one wire for the stem and the other one to support the edge of the leaf, so it will stand out (see Fig. a).
- After making the leaves, wrap the leaf stems to varying lengths, from 1½" (3.7 cm) to 3" (7.5 cm) with dark green wool.

Assembly

- First make a thick stem by winding stiff all-purpose galvanized wire with several layers of tissue paper. Next, wrap it around with green florist tape, and then arrange and attach all the florets around the top of the stem (see cross-section in Fig. c).
- Put a bunch of closed and half-open buds at the base of the flowers as shown in Fig. c and photo.
- Attach the leaves about 5" (12.5 cm) below the buds, winding down the stem with dark green wool to the bottom.

HALF-OPEN BUD

Colors: Bright red and dark green.
- Make a knot of 5 strands of red wool and attach to a florist wire stem.
- Create a closed bud around this center; part of the red wool will stick out at the top of each bud.
- Wrap down the stem of each with dark green wool as for the floret.
- Make about 5 half-open buds for each umbel.

Index